The Power Within

DISCOVERING THE PATH TO ELITE GOALTENDING

By: Mike Valley and Justin Goldman

Published Independently by Mike Valley and Justin Goldman
Cover Art and Design by Carl Herring
Interior Art by Mathew Abraham
© 2014

First Printing: 2014

ISBN-13: 9781494358846
ISBN-10: 1494358840

We would like to extend a very special thanks to the following elite goaltenders and goalie coaches for opening up to us about their personal lives as professional athletes and coaches: Richard Bachman, Niklas Backstrom, Brian Elliott, Erik Granqvist, Mitch Korn, Chris Mason, Marty Turco, Pekka Rinne, and Tomas Vokoun.

TABLE OF CONTENTS

FOREWORD

JUSTIN GOLDMAN'S MESSAGE

"A young man's deeds becomes an old man's wisdom." —*Unknown*

Over the past three years, I have been honored to call Mike Valley a mentor and close friend. So it was with great pride that I stood by his side as the co-author of his very first book.

Valley, who is the Goaltending Coach for the Dallas Stars, envisioned a single piece of literature dedicated to the process of becoming an elite goaltender. A compendium of his latest ideas and teaching points on the mental, emotional, and spiritual side of the position, this book was written to help you overcome different mental and emotional pitfalls.

Valley not only has a strong reputation as one of the best and brightest goalie coaches in hockey, but his ability to help the likes of Kari Lehtonen, Niklas Backstrom, Marty Turco, Brian Elliott, Al Montoya and many other pro goalies reach the elite status has made him a highly-respected master instructor.

Furthermore, his lessons have been revered and respected by goalies everywhere, and now many of those lessons have been published here for the sole purpose of helping you take your game to new heights.

It was back in the early stages of 2012 when Valley and I realized we were ready to co-author a book. For where I was at in my career as an independent goalie scout, working alongside an NHL goalie coach was an honor and a no-brainer. Placed in charge of editing and organizing the book, I genuinely enjoyed the experience of extrapolating and polishing his lessons, adding a few of my own lessons, conducting and transcribing the interviews, and spending endless hours refining every chapter.

With great care, I took Valley's brainchild in my hands and nurtured it through the many different stages of development.

We also believe this book was written out of sheer necessity. When our friendship reached a certain point, it was clear we both wanted to do something to eliminate the gaping void of information on these topics. We agreed the time had come for goalies of all ages and skill levels to have some sort of tangible book that was dedicated to the mental game, so we committed to making it happen. It wasn't easy, but with great support from some of the best goalie minds in the world, we went for it.

Two years later, as excited as we were to finally publish this book, we made sure to stay patient with the painstaking process. Coincidentally, "trusting the process" is one of the main lessons we discuss, a perfect twist that made us quite confident when it came time to submit the book's final proof.

While the chapters are neatly organized, this book was not the result of a specially prepared blueprint because none of these topics have been covered before in an in-depth, full-length piece of literature. The actual structure took on a life of its own; it came together in bits and pieces and at different rates and times. We had discussed these topics extensively before the idea of writing a book was even conceived, so we let the ideas and lessons naturally flow. Some of Valley's chapters originated from things he had written years ago, while some of my chapters were written after being inspired by the interviews I held with the elite goalies and goalie coaches.

Even though this was our first foray into the realm of publishing a book on goaltending, when the book was completed, we quickly realized it would not be our last. Because we thoroughly enjoyed reflecting and building upon our mutual beliefs on the mental and emotional realm of goaltending – one that is more intimate and intricate than any other position in sports – we agreed that there were still an infinite number of topics left to discuss and countless questions left to ask and answer.

Beyond the content you'll find in each chapter, our aim was to create something that goalies could use as a journal of sorts. We wanted to publish something that you could toss in your bag, or something you could read before going to bed each night, or when you're struggling to play up to your standards.

Therefore, I really believe this book was meant to be a guide, a vital map to help you discover the path of your own personal development as a goaltender. I believe it can help you become more aware of who you are as a goalie and a person, and help you determine what path you need to travel in order to begin mastering the position.

Behind the main concept of *The Three Pillars of Elite Goaltending*, I also believe this book is an elusive key that can help unlock the true power of your mind through self-reflection. It has the ability to teach you more about the way you think and feel when different situations arise in the crease. It could also act as a catalyst for your emotional growth and teach you more about so many things that simply can't be taught on the ice or on a chalkboard.

Ultimately, Mike and I started down the path of publishing this book because we felt it was time to push the envelope of the goaltender's evolution. We felt it was time to shed a different and important light on a position that is currently over-saturated by strict, rigid, and oftentimes over-complicated technique. To act as a counterweight or balancing act for the numerous tools out there that solely teach or discuss technique, we believe that this book opens the door for you to discover and embrace the forgotten and ignored mental, spiritual, and emotional realms of goaltending.

Over the years, Valley has successfully opened the eyes of many goalies to these important ideas. Because of his ability to teach these lessons to his amateur and pro students in a clear and effective way, he has turned good goalies into great goalies and great goalies into elite goalies. He understands the path one must travel in order to obtain that elusive elite status, and while a lot of these lessons are not easy to learn, you have to start somewhere.

In my own life as a goaltender and a person, Valley has played an enormous role in who I am today. Not only has he taught me endless lessons about the technical realm of goaltending, but he has injected me with the strength to believe in my own unique path. Whether it was on the ice giving me a private lesson or helping me break down video at one of his mentorship camps, Mike guided me at different times and helped transform me from a budding analyst into who I am today – a writer for NHL.com and a pro goalie scout and mentor for USA Hockey and the National Team Development Program.

My path to get to this exact moment in time has been quite unique. I grew up on a horse ranch in Texas, was suddenly introduced to the game of hockey at age 11, moved to Colorado to pursue my degree in Technical Journalism at age 18, and then I ventured into the world of radio broadcasting and print media until my pro writing and scouting career finally began in 2003.

While that path is certainly a road less-traveled, without my ability to be open and receptive to new ideas and opportunities, I would most likely still be roping cattle on a ranch in Texas. But now that I'm 31 years old and have dedicated my life to the position, I can safely say that goaltending is a calling. It's easy to find new hobbies that make you happy, but a true passion usually finds you first.

Regardless of the path you have traveled to get to where you are today, the movements and instincts displayed when you play the position were embedded deep in your bones since the moment you were born. That means you are an athlete capable of achieving whatever you dream. But you won't reach those dreams if you don't have a relentless belief in yourself and your ability to learn, grow, evolve, and trust the process.

So if there's one favor I ask of you as you prepare to read on, it would be to open up your mind. The book's lessons may seem weird or confusing at first, but is that any different from the way you felt when you strapped on the pads and pulled down the mask for the very first time?

One of my favorite quotes of all time is, "A young man's deeds becomes an old man's wisdom." The more you experience, the more you learn. The more you learn, the more capable you are of achieving success in all walks of life.

As a result, I hope this reading experience not only inspires you to play at a higher level, but teaches you something new about your own unique path towards greatness. I hope that when your eyes cross the book's final words, you will realize that you are now a stronger and more experienced goaltender.

-Goldman

PREFACE
MIKE VALLEY'S MESSAGE

Since I began my career over 20 years ago, several players, coaches, scouts, trainers, and members of the media have referred to me as the quintessential student of the game.

While it's true that my analytical skills, eye for technique, insistence on perfection and attention to detail have been necessary for advancing my profession, I believe that some of the most important things I've learned came to me not between the pipes, but in the quiet solitary moments away from the fanfare of skates, pucks and saves.

While I love the excitement and fast pace of hockey as much as (or more than) the next guy, I find that my true dedication lies not only in the study of the mechanics of the position, but also in a purposeful and mindful discovery of the intangible aspects of what makes a good goaltender great and a great goaltender elite.

This book is a journey into those intangibles – an examination of how the mind, body and spirit connects with one another and overlap to form the three unshakeable "pillars" around which inspiring and elite goaltending is built and sustained.

It has long been debated among psychologists and scientists whether it is of more benefit for us to become somewhat good at several things – a jack of all trades so to speak – or exceptionally good at just one thing. The general consensus is that a well-rounded character depends on the ability to navigate through and adapt to the ever-changing, dynamically-charged world in which we live. While I believe it is important to lead a well-balanced life, I also believe that true mastery – whether it is over an exact skill in particular or one's character in general – comes only with the desire to be exceptionally good at just one thing.

There is so much to learn along the road to mastery — strength of character, perseverance, resilience, grit, tolerance and patience just to name a few — that simply cannot be taught as well or as in-depth by flitting from one trade to the next. Taking the road less traveled and dedicating one's life to mastery over a specific set of skills often leads to a deeper understanding of one's self on a micro level, and the nature of how the world works on the universal or macro level.

Through the sharing of the ideas and concepts contained in this book, it is my intention to illustrate how the mind, body and spirit interact not only within the inner world of the individual goaltender, but also how they extend beyond the position and become the divinely inspired framework under which we all live, work and play.

Therefore, this book is as personal as it is impersonal. It is my intention that each reader sees himself contained in these pages, yet understands that his story is not unique. While the characters, setting and circumstances may differ, the theme is universal — it applies as much to goaltending as it does to any pursuit any human has taken on since the beginning of time.

Without the mind, the body will not function. Without the body, the mind has no dominion. Without the spirit, neither the mind nor the body can animate.

When these things coalesce together to create the concept of the Three Pillars of Elite Goaltending, that which is divinely inspired can be expressed through the artistic grace and beauty of this position.

I chose the crease for my expression. If you're reading this, I think you did too. Enjoy the journey!

-Valley

Introduction

The elite goaltender is like Samarium, a rare earth element that possesses great power. Impossible to fabricate in a lab and even tougher to discover, this blend of raw talent is formed in a special ecosystem over the course of many, many years.

How an elite goalie forms is the driving theme behind this book. In the search for an answer of how to create such a perfect athlete, we find time and time again that there is no standard pattern to the process of development.

But we know an elite goalie when we see one.

Pekka Rinne. Niklas Backstrom. Jonathan Quick. Kari Lehtonen. Henrik Lundqvist. Carey Price. Each of these goaltenders has a different composition and genetic makeup, but they are all beautiful pieces of art in their own unique way. We also know through years of watching them play that while they have different styles and symmetries, they play with the same goal in mind and they still share a lot of similarities.

Therefore, the aim of **The Power Within: Discovering the Path to Elite Goaltending** is to help improve your game by injecting you with some of the same knowledge and wisdom that has helped a number of NHL goaltenders reach the elite status.

We also know that you have many questions about the mental side of the goaltending position. Some of these include:

How do I bounce back from a bad goal? How do I eliminate the frustrations that come with losing a big game? How do I stay focused on the puck under pressure? How do I deal with a coach that doesn't like me? How do I avoid off-ice distractions? How do I better prepare for the biggest game of my life? Why am I always giving up goals in the same situations, even though I know what I'm doing wrong and I can do it right in practice? How come I struggle against inferior talent?

Unfortunately, there is no simple, catch-all answer for these types of questions. Instead, you must figure out for yourself how to handle each of these intimately and emotionally-charged situations.

But by showing you how a group of current elite goalies learned how to handle these same mental obstacles, it will in turn teach you more about yourself, and allow you to use their own experiences to help cultivate and develop your growing mental game. In due time, the more you understand what these elite goalies have gone through, the more you will come to understand what you need to do to play at a higher level.

So we ask that you leave the technical side of the position at the door and imagine yourself stepping into a room where your focus is solely on the mental game. Try to put yourself in a state of openness and vulnerability, a state of mind where you can be honest with who you are as a player and a person. Just like a monk prepares for a lengthy meditation, once you eliminate all distractions from your mind and focus solely on the task at hand, you will be better prepared to absorb and understand the different lessons they have kindly shared with us.

We invite you in with open arms in order to help you become a master of your own goaltending mind, and we want your reading experience to be one of positive self-growth and learning. When you've finished reading, we are confident you will have gained a deeper perspective on what it takes to go from being a raw talent to a piece of pure goaltending gold.

But be advised – this book in no way attempts to present you with a "step-by-step" list of things one must do to become elite. Instead, this book will establish a frame of reference and a solid guide for ways to refine and purify your mental approach.

You already know that being a goalie isn't easy. Things get complicated when it comes to the mental side of the position, and while the older you get the more questions you may have, eventually you will begin to find the answers inside yourself.

This complex and cumbersome aspect of the position has been largely ignored and overlooked by the general hockey community. That is to be expected since the entire process of becoming an elite mental athlete is nebulous and shrouded in the mystery of an individual's inner experiences.

But that won't stop us from drawing you a map. We wrote this book because we wanted to push forward in the search for the answers. By doing so, we can bring more balance to what we know the position represents. It is not all about angles and save selections. If it was, we'd all be making a living stopping pucks. So even though we don't have all the answers, it's time to start searching for them in the best way we know how.

As a result, this book helps you crack the code of an elite goaltender's mind by giving you a much better understanding of what their mental game is all about, why it is so difficult to master, and what you can do to simplify the complexities of being a successful goalie.

Fueled by one of the world's most intelligent goalie coaches, and with the assistance of a loyal goalie student and scout, this book sheds light on what it truly takes to be an elite netminder through more than 20 lessons compiled in digestible chapters that can be revisited and re-learned in ways that bring new meaning to your game every time you read it.

At the end of the day, **The Power Within** brings value to goalies of all ages, sizes and skill. Whether you're a coach or a parent or a player or a beer-leaguer, reading about some of the learned experiences and life lessons of an elite group of goaltenders will instill you with a certain amount of knowledge and wisdom you simply won't find anywhere else.

Before You Get Started...

Before you get started, we feel it is very important to lay out a few "rules of engagement" as you begin to read Chapter 1.

First of all, please understand that this book is not for everyone. Some of the topics we cover teeter on the edge of the taboo. They are deep; they take a certain level of openness and inner belief in things that stem beyond the visible and technical realm of goaltending. The concept of the *Three Pillars of Elite Goaltending* is not tangible in form, but rather a method used to visualize and explain the inner sanctum of who you are as a person and an athlete. It will take patience and willingness on your behalf in order to understand how some of these things can and will influence your game and your ability to compete.

Secondly, depending on your age and experience level, some of these lessons will be very simple to comprehend. Others, however, will be much tougher to follow, especially if you don't happen to play the position at a higher level, or if you are still very young. But the older you get and the more experience you gain, the more you will begin to realize that these lessons are very vital and quite worthwhile to your overall development.

Thirdly, regardless of this book's audience and regardless of who you are, where you came from, or how long you've been stopping pucks, we can guarantee that it is chock full of concepts and ideas that many elite goaltenders have implemented into their own game. Nothing within this book is made up mysticism or "hocus-pocus" fabrications. They are vital components to an elite goalie's mental and emotional development.

So whether you're a 15-year-old just beginning to discover your lifelong passion for the position, or you are a 40-year-old coach that has been playing and teaching for decades, remember one thing above all else; *be patient with the process*. Read this book with an open mind, but more importantly, give the lessons time to resonate and marinate.

It took elite goalies years and years of thinking and habit-forming and training to implement these lessons into their own game. In fact, some are still trying to learn these things, while others were never able to fully grasp them at all. Therefore you must be prepared for the same type of learning experience. Do not get frustrated if things don't stick or if you continue to fail in areas you work towards fixing. Every elite goalie will tell you that training the mind is the same type of process as training the body – experience is the key. It is only through grueling years of work that you finally reach the peak of performance.

But if you can remain patient and poised and continue to read these chapters with an open mind and a willingness to reflect on what we have to say, we guarantee that you will not only become a better goalie, but you'll also have a significant and substantial edge on your competition.

This book offers you an opportunity that very few goalies have ever received. In your hands, right here and right now, you have an opportunity to gain a much better understanding of what elite goalies experienced along their paths of development. Combined with the teachings of an elite NHL goalie coach, you are being imparted with the rare wisdom and knowledge of those that have mastered the position.

So whether you borrowed this book from a friend or stumbled across it on a website, just like we were called to write this book, so too were you called to read it. Do so with an open mind. Be receptive, be adaptive, be creative, and above all else, be thirsty for the knowledge this book has to offer.

But again we want to reinforce the fact that this book is not for everyone. What works for some goalies does not work for others, and some may simply not find any new information in the lessons we discuss in this book.

This book goes a long way in proving that the mental approach of every goaltender is a true art. No two minds work the same, and as you will read, there is unbelievable beauty behind the unique messages and lessons the elite goalies reflect in their interviews. Every goalie had a different way of painting the same type of theme on their own blank canvas.

Ultimately, just like they were able to do over the course of many years, discovering the path to elite goaltending means finding the right approach that works for you and your unique situation. The brain is a muscle that incorporates the mind, and the muscle memory needed to be an elite goaltender takes years and years to accomplish. And just like writing this book, it will be a painstaking, time-consuming process.

Chapter 1

PREPARING FOR THE LESSONS

"Flow is a harmonious experience where mind and body are working together effortlessly, leaving the person feeling that something special has just occurred. This is because flow lifts experience from the ordinary to the optimal, and it is in those moments that we feel truly alive and in tune with what we are doing."
—Susan A. Jackson and Mihaly Csikszentmihalyi, Flow in Sports

While the purpose of this book is to provide you with a deeper understanding of an elite goalie's mental approach, it is important to note that exhibiting and emulating a similar approach will not happen overnight. It takes years of practice, self-reflection, and most importantly, patience and dedication.

This book will provide you with a plethora of tools and teaching points on different topics, but transforming into a true mental warrior can only happen through years of different experiences. Over time, however, you will discover which tools work for you and which ones don't. As you continue to develop your mental and technical game, and with this book acting as a guide along the way, you will become more aware of who you are as an athlete from an emotional, mental, spiritual, and competitive point of view.

But before you begin to read the different interviews and lessons, allow us to prepare you for the journey by providing you with a well-rounded explanation of the harmony a goalie must achieve in order to reach the elite status.

Harmony, in simple terms, is referred to as Balance, or in the case of this book, Flow. In terms of goaltending, we may define "Flow" as a mutual agreement between the five senses and three dimensions during any type of competitive experience. In terms of being an athlete in any sport, harmony is often coined as the fulfilling result of peak performance.

When elite goalies are truly harmonious, everything they do is precise, accurate, and technically sound. It is movement in the purest form, devoid of all noise, hesitation, rigidness, or tension. They read plays perfectly, they don't react a moment too soon or a moment too late, pucks seem to stick to them, pads are sealed to the ice perfectly, and they display a sense of fluid grace with every save they make.

The art of becoming an elite goalie, however, is not an exact or precise science. There are an infinite number of ways to achieve that harmonious flow, and your mission is to find the most effective path that works for you.

In order to achieve flow, an elite goalie discovers through years of experience within the different stages of development that there are three elements or "pillars" that must work together in a balanced and efficient manner.

Those three pillars are *Mind, Body and Spirit.*

As the driving forces behind reaching the elite status, the different ways in which they mutually benefit each other is the true underlying theme found within each chapter.

In order to give you a visual representation of how the Three Pillars of Elite Goaltending work together, we've designed the Venn diagram below. We suggest you print this out and place it in a journal, or someplace easy for you to find.

THE THREE PILLARS
OF
ELITE GOALTENDING

The three pillars were arranged with a specific purpose in mind: to reinforce the book's message before you read the interviews and lessons. We then dissected each pillar in the next two chapters in order to put your mind in a state of true readiness. Through this 360-degree explanation of exactly what an elite goalie's mental approach is trying to achieve, you will be fully prepared to read the rest of the book.

Simply put, the Three Pillars of Elite Goaltending is the Ying to your technique's Yang. In order to achieve flow, your mind must establish a harmonious relationship with the way your body moves and reacts. They can't interfere with each other, but rather they must work together in order to achieve and reach that elusive "effortlessness" and "simplicity" we all seek throughout our lives as goaltenders.

This Venn diagram was carefully constructed through the eyes of an elite goalie coach. It was made to represent many years of dissecting the learned experiences of goalies at all levels and ages, and many of those lessons will be revealed to you in this book. It is this collection of elusive lessons that allows you to recognize the same things (both elements you are missing or already have) in your own game. It is all part of the process that is the art of becoming an elite goaltender.

As a result of reading this book, we believe that the process will be easier for you to accomplish by helping you draw parallels and establish synchronicities between the mental and technical realms of your own game. No matter how hard you try, you simply can't reach the elite status without building and maintaining three strong, sturdy pillars that work together.

When a younger, inexperienced goalie plies his trade, the three pillars interact with each other in different ways and in different situations. Like a nebulous liquid, those situations will cause the pillars to shift in weight and change in value and importance. But for visual purposes, and with the idea of flow and harmony acting as our ultimate goal, all three pillars are represented as being the same size and carrying the same weight.

Now that you know why we created this Venn diagram, below is a quick explanation of its parts, and how the different parts encompass the purpose of this book.

When the Mind and Body interact harmoniously, Rhythm is achieved. Rhythm is achieved when these two pillars work together to create successful technical goaltending. You all know what it's like to watch a goalie in a good rhythm, and if you play, you also know what being in a good rhythm feels like.

When the Body and Spirit interact harmoniously, Confidence is created. Confidence is that elusive emotion or sense of awareness that comes from knowing you are doing things the right way, and from experiencing moments where positive results occur.

Scientists and psychologists debate whether or not Confidence is the cause or effect of doing the right thing, but either way, it is an emotion we experience that can fuel further success. So we don't concern ourselves with which is which, we simply just want to create the feeling of it, sustain it, and understand the ways in which it can ebb and flow.

When the Spirit and Mind interact harmoniously, Faith and Belief flourishes. Faith is the ability of a goalie to internally motivate themselves to achieve success without having to move a muscle. It's done through the power of the mind and the spirit.

When a goalie achieves harmony with the three pillars and generates a balanced amount of Rhythm, Confidence and Faith, Flow is achieved. All elite goalies know how to establish balance between the three pillars in order to achieve this Flow.

When an elite goalie achieves flow, they establish optimal awareness and energy levels, which allows them to simply play without thinking. It is this thoughtlessness that enhances their read-and-react skills and provides them with the ability to make saves under pressure, or saves they may not normally make.

Flow is also the elite goalie's ability to recognize and process a situation without conscious thought. They are able to naturally avoid distractions, mental noise and obstacles, no matter when or where they occur, or without thinking about how to actually handle those performance pitfalls. It just happens.

So there you have it; the Three Pillars of Elite Goaltending, with Flow in the middle. Flow is achieved by having a pristine and harmonious interaction of all three pillars, and in doing so, it creates a feeling of wholeness, because you play naturally without one pillar supporting another one more than the other.

We'll learn more about these topics in future chapters, but this is the fundamental cornerstone of this book's purpose, which is to help you learn how to achieve mental clarity and emotional readiness. Once you understand the concept of the Venn diagram, this book will open doors for you to learn from its lessons and achieve peak performance on a more consistent basis, regardless of the situation you are in, or despite the personal struggles you may be dealing with at any given moment.

As we continue to prepare you for the interviews and lessons, now that we have explained how the Three Pillars of Elite Goaltending connect and intertwine, we also need to stress the importance of how all three exist and act as separate entities.

Your body is everything that encompasses what your brain tells you to do. Your body includes your muscles, bones, your level of flexibility, agility, foot speed, and more.

Your mind is the analytical side of processing the information needed to play the position. It is not only the stabilizer (proprioception) of movements, but the machine that converts stimuli to visual responses in any given situation or moment.

It includes the brain, which is a highly specialized supercomputer capable of processing extremely large amounts of information at the speed of light. Neurons snap and spark and the brain tells your muscles to move your bones.

The brain also includes all conscious thoughts and all subconscious movements. From the frontal lobe to the stem, it is an amazing piece of equipment, and the result of millions of years of human evolution.

Your spirit is a reflection of your emotional state as an athlete. It is your passion and desire to achieve greatness. It is your memory of collected experiences, your idealistic dreams, and your urge to live each day with a true purpose. It is a re-living of past experiences that are similar to what you may currently experience, and the warm feeling you get when you know you're on the right path.

With these simple definitions of your mind, body and spirit at the forefront of the next chapter, we continue to prepare you for the book's lessons by looking at the role of each pillar from a goaltender's point of view.

Chapter 2

THE ROLE OF THE BODY AND MIND

In Chapter 1, we revealed that the path to becoming an elite goaltender includes the process of reaching a state of harmony or flow. We explained this process through the carefully constructed concept of the _Three Pillars of Elite Goaltending_.

But in order for you to create the balance needed to reach Flow, there's no denying that you must treat your body like a temple. If you don't, the pillars will eventually begin to lack the strength and stability needed to support each other. As time goes on, your health and your athleticism will deteriorate.

The old adage "your body is a temple" exists because it is considered to be the sacred house that shelters your brain, which is the vital organ that gives your five senses the power to process and experience everything this world has to offer. If you don't take care of your body, you don't stay healthy. If you don't stay healthy, you reduce your mind's ability to assist your body in performing at the highest level possible.

In the realm of goaltending, an unhealthy body will reduce reaction speeds, tighten key muscles like the groin and hamstrings, hinder the ability to track pucks, and diminish your ability to move with power and control at the key moments.

Like a dancer or a gymnast, you must learn how to pay very close attention to the different biological signs that reveal information about the way you move when performing or feel when preparing to play. The daily routine of how you live, eat, sleep and treat your body becomes a major role player in establishing the connection between your physical and mental states. This includes your ability to maintain or alter your mood, attitude, confidence, and more importantly, your ego.

While there are many roles the body has when it comes to influencing the way you perform, we chose to focus on one area in particular – nutrition.

Nutrition continues to gain importance in the role of a goaltender's development because if you don't fuel your body with the right foods, you won't get the right results. Simply put, if all you eat is junk food, your body will work like junk. You are what you eat, and in today's world, which is full of processed and commercialized food, it is more important than ever to eat balanced and healthy or "clean" foods.

Nutrition has become so important for elite athletes over the last few years that many personal trainers are beginning to learn more about an area of study known as Nutritional Therapy.

Nutritional Therapy is a specific approach to treating medical, physical, and emotional conditions (and their associated symptoms) through the use of certain foods or specially tailored diets. By altering or improving an athlete's diet, they reduce the risk of developing complications in certain conditions such as diabetes, dehydration, muscle spasms, asthma, and even pre-existing or more prevalent issues like high cholesterol.

For an athlete, Nutritional Therapy not only includes the biochemical aspect of their blood with their specific conditions or symptoms, but it also includes the study of how to enhance an already healthy and active body. A nutritional therapist can help runners breathe better, swimmers improve their lung capacity, reduce the amount of lactic acid buildup in a hockey player's body, and they can even help a goalie stay focused, flexible and hydrated for longer periods of time.

As scientists learn more about the importance of the food we consume, Nutritional Therapy continues to reach further into the depths of our body's ability to process those foods in order to enhance our health and athletic performance. In fact, numerous studies in the field have revealed that not only can the food you eat influence how your genes express themselves, but so can your internal and external environment.

For example, drinking too much caffeine is a type of addiction that can alter your mood. The same goes for alcohol, or on the flip side, green "super-foods" that can provide the body with healthy bacteria that helps you build cleaner muscles and tissues, or aid in the fight against diseases and illnesses.

As a result of the progress scientists have made in the field of Nutritional Therapy, we now know that food can often be better medicine than drugs. The body will heal itself if you put the right things into it, so you must be careful with what you consume – food is capable of changing your genetic makeup and the way you act.

For the goaltender, this is more than enough proof to realize that your body is a temple, and everything from the amount of sleep you get to the way you recover from a workout will influence the role your body and mind play in the development of your skills and your mental approach.

While we could spend a whole chapter discussing the role the body plays in becoming an elite goaltender, most of it is fairly obvious. The older you get, the more important a pure and pristine body becomes. If you want more information on the topic of nutrition, we suggest you discuss Nutritional Therapy with your trainer, P.E. teacher, doctor, or anyone else that has a background in exercise science.

The Role of the Mind

Scientists have come to learn through years of study and research that our minds have amazing control over our bodies.

Each action we make, whether voluntary or involuntary, begins in the mind. Throughout the day, and even when we sleep, our brains are busy assimilating information and formulating directives to keep our bodies functioning in ways that are the most optimal for survival.

Thousands upon thousands of neural passages begin in the brain and spinal cord and weave their way through our bodies to create an intricate network of cells. This information superhighway, which is completely contained within the human body, would stretch for 45 miles if it was laid end-to-end. It requires little, if any, effort on our part to function. If something goes wrong, our bodies immediately and subconsciously begin repairing the damage, regardless of what our conscious brains are telling us.

Normal brain function consumes nearly one-fifth of the total energy required by our bodies each day. So the brain not only helps our bodies produce and metabolize energy, it also consumes a portion of the very energy it creates.

The amazing powerhouse that is the human body is fueled by the foods we eat, the air we breathe and the water we drink. It is conditioned by our movement: the exercises and stretches we perform to keep ourselves strong, flexible and healthy. It is refreshed and re-energized while we sleep.

As we explained above, all of these things are necessary for us to survive as humans in this engaging and multi-faceted environment we call Planet Earth. But let's dig a little deeper and tie the role of the mind to the developing goaltender.

What is it, exactly, that controls our minds? If the brain is the central processor for the body, who or what is responsible for directing the brain? If the brain is the hardware, where did the software come from? Where does the energy that generates the mind's power come from?

Unlike computers, which must be designed and programmed by a team of tech savvy engineers, the brain appears to function on its own. There is no software developer, no hardware manufacturer, and no tech support to call when something goes awry. There is only the brain, all alone, sitting atop its temple, the body.

Traditional science, medicine, and the study of physiology and anatomy lead us to believe that the brain, and its network of nerve cells, is all that's required for the body to function. We also know from the study of human evolution that the brains of early humans were much less evolved than those of humans today. The fossil records show, and many scientists believe, that the human species began to diverge from apes when their brains became large enough to allow for things like tool making and language development.

However, in order for something to grow, a seed must first be planted. So, in the case of the human brain, what, or where, is that seed? Which anatomical feature of the human brain is responsible for the continuum of growth and development that occur on an individual level and across an entire species?

Maybe the answer lies within the ability for the advanced human to eventually grasp the concept of the spirit. This discovery of a higher source of power and energy allowed us to create an individualized sense of identity. It is this creation of a spirit that helped us tap into areas of the brain and mind that were eventually hidden and shut off from the supercomputer.

But none of that is possible without a mind to process these concepts.

For those that want to become an elite goaltender, you must first understand that the role of the mind is to allow the body to move without any noise or distraction interfering with the ability to achieve Flow. So many things can pull us away from playing at our best, whether it be personal, atmospheric, or uncontrollable. Therefore, your goal is to run certain processes in the brain that allow your conscious mind to shut off, which will then allow the subconscious mind to control the inner panel of your body.

Once goalies begin to play at a competitive level, they often hear the phrase "Paralysis by Analysis." This mantra points to the important concept that the more we actually make conscious thoughts in the crease, the more likely we are to over-think situations and lack the timing or rhythm needed to make the big save. It is usually at the moment of thinking consciously about what to do next that the puck is whizzing past us.

But by training the body rigorously and consistently, muscle memory develops, and that allows the mind to move the body more effectively, and in a more subconscious manner.

We go into more detail about the role of the mind for the elite goaltender later in the book, but the main subject is simple; we must learn to play the position without having to purposely think at all. We must train the body to let it work without interference, and this only comes with years of highly specialized training.

But even a very young or inexperienced goaltender with average talent has the ability to play without mental noise. In fact, you will read a very special story from an elite goalie coach about the beauty of children, and how they are able to play without any pressures or mental noise because they play the position for the sheer enjoyment of playing with friends and stopping the puck.

It is this child-like state of mind that elite goalies are able to reach, because they understand the role the mind plays when it comes to executing their technique in a competitive environment.

This proves that even *you* have the ability to achieve "Flow" and out-perform someone else with more skill, but only after you learn how to control your mind and your thoughts when it matters most. Whether or not the physical body has the capacity to make flawless saves at an elite level matters not, because as you will learn in ensuing chapters, it's all in how you prepare yourself to play the game.

You play some of the best hockey in your life when you're happy. On occasion, the role of the mind is to embrace that state of happiness. When you remind yourself that having fun and being happy is the most important goal of today's practice or game, the mind is influencing the body in a manner that allows you to smile, relax, and ultimately play at a higher level.

Your body and your technical skills may have their limits, but your mind is limitless, and it is much more powerful than you may have possibly imagined.

Chapter 3

THE ROLE OF THE SPIRIT

When it comes to traversing down the tricky trail of developing your game, today's goaltenders arguably face the most stressful and complicated emotional obstacles of any previous era.

The influence and rising prominence of social media, the importance of managing one's public identity and reputation, the inescapable political nuances between coaches and parents, various forms of bullying, and the increased competition between friends can lead many younger goalies to experience unforeseen levels of stress, and in some cases, pure burnout.

In order to combat these performance killers, you should first learn to understand exactly what role the spirit plays in the process of becoming an elite goalie. Not only can this pillar help eliminate stress and performance anxiety, it can also help boost low levels of confidence, reinforce your purpose and goals, and even improve your pre-game preparation skills.

Those are only a few of the endless benefits that the spirit could play in your development. But what exactly is the goaltender's definition of the spirit?

For starters, the spirit fills the space between your body and mind and serves as the ultimate control center for your feelings. It is the layer of invisible mental "soil" that gives birth to your emotions and helps them bloom. These emotions are then quickly and effortlessly labeled by the brain so that your conscious mind (and then your physical body) can assimilate, organize, and process the information accordingly.

Simply put, your spirit is a special blueprint that your identity designs over time to reflect who you are as a goalie and an athlete. It is a collection of your reflections of every experience you have ever had as a player and a person. Your spirit is also your willingness to believe that something greater than your own physical abilities exists within you. It is often considered a divine presence or the inner fuel that generates the motivation needed to achieve everything you desire or long to become.

Since it is not a tangible tool, goalies must learn how to acknowledge and "activate" the spirit in order for it to help you along the path of becoming an elite goaltender. In order to accomplish this, at some point in time, you must take a leap of faith and have the courage to believe in that which you cannot see.

You can certainly enhance your knowledge of the spirit by taking it upon yourself to research what the spirit means in a wider scope beyond sports. Or you can also discover the role of the spirit by trusting that something beyond the realm of the body and mind is there to help enhance your skills.

But from the personal point of view of an elite NHL goalie coach, Mike Valley explains one way to activate the spirit with this statement:

"The elite goalie must believe in the existence of a universal source of energy that endows each of us as a special, graceful athlete with the capacity to grow, change, evolve, and adapt at any given moment."

As Valley explains throughout this book, nowhere are the three pillars of goaltending more connected than at the elite level (of any sport). This is especially true for the pro goaltender because they are subjected to more mental noise from both external (fans and media) and internal pressures (ego and their own expectations).

"The goaltender is alone on an island, a man trapped within his mind, left to experience the game on his own accord," Valley continued. "We move, react, and process game information in our own unique ways, and we do this without realizing that there's an internal, inherent force guiding our mind's hands."

So to wrap it up in a tidy and digestible sentence, activating the spirit is simply flipping a mental switch and becoming aware and cognizant that there is something very powerful within us.

If you are capable of believing in things you can't necessarily see, understanding the role of the spirit is a lesson that is neither difficult nor far-fetched. If you are more of a "seeing is believing" personality type, that is fine, but you may struggle to understand or believe in what Valley is trying to explain.

Either way, when a goaltender reaches the elite status, they inevitably learn how necessary it is to have a strong spirit.

Those that do become aware of their spirit's influence on their personal development will find it easier to lean on this constant source of inspiration in their daily lives. They will rarely ever experience burnout because the spirit strives for and helps bring a life into balance. They will be more inclined to put in the extra effort needed to out-train and out-compete their opponents because the spirit always wants to win. They will be more consistent with their approach and their motivation will never wane when the going gets tough.

An elite goalie with a strong spirit is the seed of their own personal growth as an athlete. They achieve harmony and flow with more ease because their passion promotes their success. Work is still considered fun, losing is considered as a slight bump in the road, giving up bad goals is considered part of the process, and winning is considered as one small step in the right direction. Valley also sums it up with this quote:

"An elite goalie has achieved balance with their spirit when it acts as a quiet and steady force through all of the highs, lows and obstacles that come with the territory of playing a professional sport for a living. The spirit acts as a guide to help them be even-keeled with their emotions, never getting too high when they're playing great and never getting too low when things aren't going their way. It is this wide perspective of life — realizing that hockey is just a game — that allows a goalie to stay centered and focused on what matters most in any given moment."

To take the role of the spirit one step further, it is important to understand that an elite goaltender's talents are a charism.

When life blesses an athlete with an extraordinary gift or skill, the spirit eventually teaches them that their gift is not solely for them. Rather, the gift exists for them to use in a manner that helps, supports, and inspires others.

So if you are a young goaltender with "gifted" raw skills, always appreciate the fact that those gifts were given to you for a purpose. And when you understand that the ultimate purpose of your gift is to help your team win or to make your parents happy or to teach others how to play the position better, then you will begin to play with a discernment of spirit.

The "discernment of spirit" sounds complicated, but it simply means knowing that whatever talents or gifts you have are not yours alone. You played a key role in honing the tools needed to execute and display that gift, but since goaltending is a skill that includes so many natural gifts like flexibility, reflexes and reaction speed, it reflects a grace far beyond the technical realm. The senses needed to be elite goalies are tied to the subconscious level, whether it is the enhanced vision needed to read plays, catch pucks, or track the trajectory of a puck being launched off a shooter's blade.

When an elite goalie understands that their extraordinary gifts are not a direct result of their own work, but the work of something beyond their own consciousness, they become a humble athlete and rarely fall victim to their own ego. A humble goaltender has an open mind, open heart, and lacks any sense of an ego because they play for the pure love of stopping pucks and for the sheer purpose of competing and trying to win.

The next step is to discover the purpose of having this gift. Ask yourself, what exactly do you use it for? Do you use it for the sake of stroking your own ego and increasing your own power and prestige? Or do you use it how it was meant to be used; to help and enlighten others? Do you stop pucks for your own glory, to gain more individual accolades, or to get approval from your coach and teammates? Or do you use it because you truly love and enjoy being a part of the recipe needed for a team to win?

Hockey is the ultimate team sport, but many goalies are susceptible to developing an inflated ego because they learn at a young age that they are alone in the crease and that they are the last line of defense. While this is true (like Valley said earlier, goalies are alone on an island), the discernment of spirit will always bring you back to the realization that winning and losing is not the direct result of your actions alone, but the result of being a part of a team effort.

With the team at the forefront of your mind, once you have the discernment of spirit and you know your skills are a charism and a gift, anytime you accomplish something special, you will experience that humility and others will appreciate you, because you know you didn't do it all on your own.

"It is so easy to praise yourself when you win a game or make a great save, so it really takes guts to give all of the credit to someone besides yourself," Valley said. "Yet at the elite level, you will constantly hear goalies downplay their own skills and deflect the praise towards their teammates."

As you can see, part of the process of becoming an elite goaltender is believing in something beyond yourself, even when there is no reason to believe in it. The passion of playing the position provides you with a certain belief system, but when you begin to believe that you are the alpha and omega of everything, you no longer respect the charism and grace of your talents. To think you are the center of your own universe will inflate your ego to the point it hinders the role of your spirit. You have to be willing to believe in something more.

An elite goalie is always aware that, while they clearly have a great talent, even when their talent is in the spotlight or the center of attention, there are other people and things worth thanking and appreciating. It may be lonely in the crease and it may be tough to handle the pressure of being a culprit or a scapegoat, but even then, you are never truly alone.

This "blind faith" not only proves you can be a humble teammate, it can also give you the courage needed to face and overcome whatever internal or external fears or obstacles you may be facing.

Courage is experiencing the fear of pain or failure, but still strapping on the pads and giving it your best effort anyways. Without courage, a goalie will always succumb to fear. The puck is dangerous, the game is dangerous, and it is usually when you begin to fear the puck that you hesitate or make yourself more prone to injury.

Without a doubt, the concept and feeling of fear is one of the biggest hurdles a goalie faces during their development. But at the same time, it is a necessary component of becoming elite because it allows the spirit to strengthen your sense of courage as time goes on.

Goalies have nowhere to hide, so while you could certainly fail all the time, your spirit provides you with the ability to go out and play right through that sense of fear. And regardless of the results, you come out the other side a little bit stronger and a little more experienced than before.

This "trial by fire" is how the learning and maturing process takes place, and that maturing process is how an elite goalie learns to persevere through the trials and tribulations of a career. Eventually, when things start to go their way and they do experience the highs, they remain humble because they know they are susceptible to experiencing the despair of the lows at any moment.

Like fear, despair is a serious emotional pitfall in sports because it blocks the spirit from playing its intended role. Despair sets in when you allow yourself to believe that no matter what you do, nothing will change and you will always suffer bad results. On the flip side, having too much pride takes place when you think that, regardless of the results, everything you've done is so great because you did it all on your own.

Regardless of fear or despair, frustration or failure, the spirit has the power to erase all of those pitfalls, reducing them to the point where they are merely minor bumps along the road.

The role of the spirit is so multi-faceted and intricately laced into who we are as athletes and human beings that it is a vital part of the process of becoming an elite goalie.

Everyone will have a different definition of the spirit, how to "activate" it, and what role it plays in the process of development, but all that matters is that you realize every goalie at every age and skill level has the power to use their spirit in a positive way. It's merely a matter of flipping the right switches in the panel of your inner body in order to begin establishing the balance needed to achieve Flow.

The spirit is a spark that ignites your passion for goaltending and brushes away the dust and debris that interferes with your ability to play with a clear and confident mind. It is the invisible yet omnipresent force that turns your body into a piece of graceful art. For these and many other reasons, it will forever play a key role in your ability to become an elite goaltender.

Chapter 4

WHY GOALTENDING IS 90% MENTAL

"Despite the many long years of instruction and practice that most athletes put in, they generally act spontaneously when they make outstanding plays. The conscious knowledge of correct and incorrect moves serves as kindling and logs to a fire, but in the white heat of the event they are burnt into nonexistence, as the reality of the flames takes over – flames originating in a source beyond conscious know-how, melding athlete, experience, and play into a single event."
–Michael Murphy and Rhea A. White, In the Zone: Transcendent Experience in Sports

"Goaltending is 90-percent mental."

This is one of the truly iconic phrases you hear from goalie coaches everywhere. At the elite level, some coaches even believe the percentage is more like 98. But why is this considered to be a fundamental truth for goaltenders? What makes goaltending so much more "mental" than positions in other sports?

Goaltending is 90-percent mental because what your body must accomplish in order to be successful on a consistent basis isn't possible without the strength of the other two pillars – your mind and spirit.

More than any other position in sports, goaltenders are prone to suffering from a plethora of athletic anxiety disorders. These include muscle soreness, trembling, restlessness, irritability, fatigue, shortness of breath, uncontrollable sweating, bouts of random dizziness, and for some even more extreme anxiety like nausea, vomiting, speechlessness, and OCD.

Being "on edge" is par for the course before a big game because of the pressures that come with being the most important player on the ice. As the last line of defense, a goalie stands alone and has nowhere to hide. Left to their own devices, goalies naturally try to cope with these disorders and protect themselves from fear and shame in different ways, many of which can lead to even more psychological issues.

The prevalence of anxiety, simple phobias, excessive superstitions, obsessive-compulsive disorders, and post-traumatic stress disorders are fairly common in pro goaltenders. Furthermore, knowing that the mind is such a powerful tool, it can also counter-attack itself and work against you.

It is only through years of honing and executing a myriad of mental skills like focus, pre-game visualization, managing fear and negative thoughts, and the ability to quiet the mind that a goalie can harness the true power of their technical and physical skills.

Without knowing how to execute these mental skills, goalies lack the ability to control how they act, react, and play when they are forced to perform in stressful, uncomfortable, or pressure-filled situations. As a result, they often fail to perform up to their standards because they don't have the confidence or wherewithal to do what they normally do in comfortable situations. Goalies that lack a strong mental game spend too much energy trying to discern or ignore the negative external and internal threats that can exist in any given situation. From there, frustration casts a shadow over their minds because they know they have the potential, but they can't ascertain or explain why certain keys no longer fit certain locks.

As time goes on, however, goalies naturally learn through sheer experience the importance of developing their mental game alongside their technical game. They start to understand for themselves the same thing we portray in the concept of the Three Pillars of Elite Goaltending, and they begin to reflect on things more from an internal point of view.

In order to connect our concept of the three pillars to the traditional learning experience, we can use a very common model to explain how a developing goaltender becomes more aware of the importance of their mental approach. This acts as a more concrete answer as to why the position eventually becomes 90-percent mental, all the while giving you a solid visual representation of the many topics discussed in this book.

This model, which is often called the **Four Stages of Development**, is used in many walks of life and can be applied to just about any type of athletic or professional trade. Below is a basic explanation of the four stages along with an application to the path of becoming an elite goaltender.

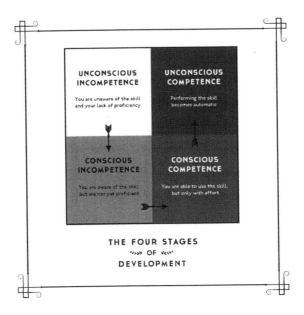

THE FOUR STAGES
OF
DEVELOPMENT

Author's Note: You will notice that there are no ages tied to the four stages. The reason for this is due to the fact that goalies are introduced to the position at different ages and every goalie's mind develops at a different rate and in different ways. No two minds learn the complex physiological movements of goaltending at the same rate, and therefore categorizing the four stages into age groups is a fallacy. Parts of the explanations below were originally published by Justin Goldman on The Goalie Guild in July, 2012.

Stage 1 – Unconscious Incompetence: The initial stage of development begins at the moment we first strap on the pads. During this stage, we usually have no idea what we're doing and we have no idea of how little we know about playing the position. This is either due to the fact we're too young to consciously process what is happening, or we've simply never done it before. We may have seen other goalies play, but since the act of wearing pads and facing shots is such an unfamiliar and foreign feeling, we are incompetent when it comes to executing the skills needed, and we're also totally unaware of what we're doing when we actually try to do it.

Think back to your first time on the ice or your first time in pads. You had no idea how to butterfly, you just dropped down and tried to look like your favorite goalie. You never knew how to hold your glove, you just held it in a way that was natural for your specific body type. You stood there and let pucks hit you, and you probably had no clue how to control your edges or even how to skate up and down the ice.

We've all been through this awkward stage of development before, and as we began to spend more time in our gear, we became more conscious of our movements, and more competent when making the movements.

Stage 2 – Conscious Incompetence: As we get older, we begin to gain a better understanding of the position. We also begin to execute the basic and intermediate components of technique. We understand what a shuffle and a T-Push are, we understand how to hold our gloves and stick properly, and we begin to learn how important it is to skate well.

But in this stage, we are still incompetent at executing the movements fluidly. We have not yet developed any type of muscle memory, so while we are conscious (aware) of what we need to do, we can't really do it yet (incompetence) in a consistent or biomechanically efficient manner.

Many goalies that begin to play goal at an older age will actually begin their development in this stage, for while they have been watching goalies perform long enough to know what a goaltender needs to do to stop the puck, they have no experience doing it with their own body. Therefore, the focus of this stage is on learning the movements and executing them enough times to begin developing muscle memory.

Stage 3 – Conscious Competence: In the third stage of goaltending development, we become aware of what we need to do, and while we're clearly aware of how to do it, we have to exert higher amounts of mental energy in order to execute properly. This stage is centered around one's unique cognitive skills, as we process information (whether by watching other goalies do it or through sheer "hands on" instruction from coaches) and display the ability to duplicate it on our own.

An example of conscious competence would be seen in the execution of a power slide in an intermediate goalie, or their understanding of positioning and angles. While they know how to execute the movements or where to stand in the crease, while they can do it successfully, they have to put in a considerable amount of thought and energy in order to do it correctly.

They have to think about it in order to make sure they are activating the appropriate muscles (or parts of their memory), and using the proper techniques to execute it with success.

Stage 4 – Unconscious Competence: In the final stage of goalie development, years of muscle memory and pattern recognition, plus many years of improved body awareness leads the goalie to execute the position automatically, or without consciously thinking about what they're doing. They are unconsciously performing technical elements like butterfly recoveries, power slides, rotations, half-butterfly saves and more.

This is the stage we all strive to enter, and this is the stage where all pro-level and elite goalies exist. They are creatures that act on impulse and react to patterns and stimuli in ways that take little or no cognitive thought at all. Their bodies are programmed to react in certain ways, and the evolution of their vision, reflexes, and sheer instincts allow them to be extremely successful.

———

As you can see, the Four Stages of Development is a great way to explain how we evolve as athletes, and how the mind helps the body develop the skills and mechanics needed to be a successful goalie.

What makes this model so interesting is the route a goalie takes to move from one stage to the next. As you will soon realize, no two paths are the same and no two goalies spend the same amount of time in each stage.

Every goalie is different, and that's what makes this model such a great tool for self-reflection and personal growth. Take some time to write down your experience in each of the four stages. Which stage are you currently in? What can you do to enter the next stage?

Furthermore, this model can be applied individually to different elements of the position. Maybe your skating skills are in one stage, while your ability to read plays and cover certain angles are in another stage. Maybe you have become very advanced at tracking aerial angles and making unconscious competent glove saves, but you struggle to execute lateral pushes, and you're still stuck in the conscious competent, or maybe even the conscious incompetent stage for that skill.

No matter how your current state of development looks, the more time you take to reflect on where your skills lie, the more aware you become of what your body and mind are doing. And the more aware you become, the more likely you are to improve your weaknesses and fortify your strengths.

The four stages of development were broken down in the technical realm as an example, so realize it can also be applied directly to the mental realm as well. As you experience growth and a deeper understanding of your technical game, the way in which you manage and cultivate your emotions play a more significant role in your development.

Therefore, a strong mental approach will slowly begin to manifest itself through a wide collection of experiences. You will begin to realize that losses are more valuable than wins, playing on bad teams is more beneficial than playing behind good teams, and going through rough patches thickens the skin.

After struggling or failing in various pressure situations, you develop more competence in how you manage your emotions. Before that, you will begin to become aware of those emotions actually playing a role in how you perform.

Unfortunately, exhibiting the conscious competence in the mental and emotional realm of goaltending on a consistent basis cannot be achieved without experience. Unless you go out and play, you can't truly learn what it takes to play at your best.

And therein lies the chance for you to discover the path to becoming an elite goaltender.

At some point in every athlete's journey, they come to the realization that talent alone is not enough. The body, which is one of the three pillars, must be able to rely on and draw from learned experience.

Goalies, especially ones that have many years of pro experience, eventually go through this sense of emotional growth and awakening. Only then do they come to learn that there is much more to the position than what you can see.

Therefore, the elite goaltender understands that they must focus most of their energy and time (the "90-percent" adage) on the mental aspects of the position, which, as you now know, also includes a harmonious connection of the spirit and body.

Just as an elite goalie comes to learn these things over time, so too will you become exposed to many of the same lessons through this book. But for now, regardless of where you are at in the development process, the ensuing chapters and interviews will broaden your horizons and illuminate the paths that other goalies have traveled during their own journey to becoming elite.

As you will find, they all learned many of the same lessons, but in very different ways. And at the end of the day, they all achieved the same thing; harmonious flow and a truly gifted understanding of how to be mental warriors at any given moment in time.

So how exactly does a group of elite goaltenders reach the final destination of their own personal journey? How do they strengthen the three pillars and establish harmony and flow in their game and lives, despite very difficult obstacles, roadblocks, and other pitfalls?

Now you're truly ready to find out.

-Goldman

Chapter 5

TALKING WITH MARTY TURCO

Author's Note: We introduce you to our collection of interviews with elite goalies with one of the more recognizable goalies over the past decade, Marty Turco. Although he is no longer playing, his career was a historic one. He's an icon in the Dallas Stars organization and he played the position in a very unique, bold, and confident way. He revolutionized the way goalies pass and handle the puck with the "Turco Grip" and he continues to influence the way smaller goalies play the position. He also happens to be one of the strongest mental warriors the goaltending position has ever seen, so his insights on how to manage the three pillars of elite goaltending is remarkably valuable in reinforcing the purpose of this book.

Goldman: Mike was really excited to have you as the first player interview in our book. He wanted you to set the stage for enlightening goalies on the path you took to become a mental warrior. I know you guys worked together when you were with the Stars and that you are still close friends today, so to start, how would you explain the way you guys shared the same ideas on having the mental fortitude needed to become elite?

Turco: "Valley and I are definitely on the same page when it comes to philosophy, so I think it goes without saying that everything we do in life as goalies is mental. You can call it mind games or you can call it a belief system or superstitions or just a way of life, but no matter what phrase or cliché you want to use, it's all a roundabout way of seeking the truth. To do something and to do it well and have the desire to do your best is one thing, but the truth is that nobody can be at their best until they're fully committed. And that's not only physically speaking, but especially mentally speaking.

If you're not committed 100-percent into it, you can never totally be at your best and you can never become an elite goalie."

Goldman: Why do you think it is so difficult for goalies to become elite mental warriors?

Turco: "Well, the unfortunate thing about goaltending is that it's an 82-game season, but the way coaches handle practices between playing all these games is a little asinine and a backwards mentality. The amount of pressure that they put on goalies combined with the value that goalies have to a team's success means that a goalie knows they have to play well all the time. Never mind the importance of a goalie just feeling good and confident about themselves, but winning is everything. Regardless of how a goalie plays one night, sometimes just 12 hours later on the morning after a game, the whole design of the practice is maybe 10-percent geared towards actually supporting the goaltender. I get the pressure the coaches are under to win, but you would think in today's day and age, practices would be more catered towards goaltenders so that they can get what they really need in order to prepare the right way. Being in this situation will inevitably take a toll after a while, and that's one of the main unfortunate things that pro goalies face as a pitfall of becoming elite, and something that is part of being involved in the ultimate team sport."

Goldman: So what was one of the most vital lessons you learned about being an elite goalie over the course of your NHL career?

Turco: "Goaltenders live on an island. We have our own set of rules, our own equipment, we get treated differently, and we speak a different language. There's really nothing like it in sports, playing this type of position and this special game on skates. But with that came the realization that a majority of my constituents and colleagues didn't even understand my position. That even includes some coaches, and I'm like, how is that even possible? You've been around goaltenders your whole life and you can't play the game without them, so how could you not understand them? Of course there are some coaches that do understand the need for them and understand the difference between the good ones and the bad ones, but even they don't really take the time to get to know or appreciate the intricate details that go into the mental capacity needed to play the position at an elite level. That's where you get the general saying, "Hey, I just want my goalies to stop the puck." And to me, goalies are always like, "Yeah, I'm trying to…" but we never tell players to just go score goals or to just go sit on the bench because you've skated long enough for now. So because we really appreciate the mental side of it, we don't dig on our teammates even though they look at us through one odd eyeball. It's a really unique relationship that goaltenders have within a super-secretive locker room that fans don't really get to see. Even within our world, we still feel like we're at odds with everyone else, or that we're just different. Not that we're alone out there, but it's already hard enough to be normal, which is why being an elite goalie can be so difficult in terms of the mental and emotional side of being an athlete."

Goldman: Is this why there are so many goalies that fail and so few that actually succeed?

Turco: "I think so. When you get to this elite level where you are on the cusp of becoming a full-time NHL goalie, just getting a chance to turn pro is such a rare feat. Even though you see goalies play differently with different skill sets and at different sizes, it's hard to predict what kind of success they will have, or who is going to be great or not, without knowing them personally or knowing a lot about their personality or their mental capacity. The guys that have been the greatest, it goes without saying that they have some of the most complex bandwidths between the ears. You want to see exactly what's in there and even then there's guys that maybe didn't have comparable talent in relation to their peers, but had a longer and more prosperous NHL career because of their ability to handle their emotions. I've seen plenty of goalies that I've played with where I wondered how good they could have been if they had their wits about them."

Goldman: Every goalie we talk to in this book is at a different stage in their playing career. But for someone like yourself that has been through a career from start to finish, what would you say to help a younger goalie gain some of the knowledge needed to handle these different obstacles without them actually going through them?

Turco: "I think for aspiring or young goalies, whether they are at the college, junior or pro level, since we know that there's nothing more valuable than pure experience, you should always have an 'open mind' concept. The 'open mind' concept falls under the general category of 'big-picture' learned experience. The big picture can sometimes be looked at every year, every summer, every month, or maybe even every day. Regardless of the scale, they just need to have a real broad sense of what has happened and chalk it up as a learning experience. When you do this, you can get over it and appreciate it and hopefully not let it happen again. You have to understand how you handled that situation mentally and how you handled it physically, like if you thought you could do something different so it doesn't happen again. But ultimately, just be sure to always appreciate the ebbs and flows, the negative and positive impacts of things that happen to you as a goalie, and then appreciate it by knowing it's an opportunity to learn what you'd like to do better. For that matter, also appreciate the good things that you do and the things you're proud of doing because that's something you have inside of you. If you can handle a certain situation or realize there's something you want to handle differently, well, just know that you can. Then it really becomes easy to look back, have a positive mindset with how you processed the experience, and then forge ahead with a solid game plan."

Goldman: Was that understanding something you learned later in your career, or was it something that was always a part of who you were before you turned pro?

Turco: "It was actually one of the things that was easier for me to achieve in my career. What was the hardest for me was the day-to-day, inside-the-game type of mentality. Especially when I was younger, this happened during the pre-goalie coach era, so I was my own goalie coach at the time, and even though I wasn't aware of these vital lessons, I always had fun with that process. I was always known as a little bit of a different goaltender. I was quick, I read and reacted to plays better than most, but technically speaking, I didn't fit a mold because I never stopped the puck the exact same way twice. But I was different and I embraced that because I knew that some of the greatest goalies ever were considered different, like the sheer unpredictability of someone like Dominik Hasek."

Goldman: So what made you mentally tough, or at least aware that you had some mental toughness, in your pre-college days?

Turco: "I think no matter what arena I was in through different stages of my life, I didn't find it difficult to be a good winner or difficult to handle things when I wasn't playing well. I was able to keep an even-keel about it, appreciate it, and move on. When things didn't go well, I just learned to try and change things up. When you do this for a living, you can look at your body and you can tweak things, whether it's how you're training, what you're doing in the gym, or what you're not doing in other areas — and obviously nowadays we even have equipment guys to help us tweak things with our gear. Those fall in the category of mind games, but if you believe in what you're doing, and your knowledge of something is growing, and you're paying attention to what your job is and how you can do it better, that's just going to add confidence, no matter what is going on. So I found out pretty early in my career that switching things up was always a pretty good method."

Goldman: How were you able to achieve that even-keeled approach? It's such an important element to a goalie's development, but for an elite goalie like yourself that was so in tune with your emotions, how did you manage them through all of the ups and downs?

Turco: "Getting scored on in games and giving up goals in practice and having guys or fans chirp or parents speak their mind, well, we're all human. It might look like goalies don't give a crap or we're not paying attention, but they have to turn around and play well and not let it bother them. That can be innate, but that can also be achieved by simply finding ways to alleviate pressure on yourself. I think the majority of that ability to alleviate pressure comes from what you think about beforehand, and what type of preparation you put into a game or situation beforehand. I really believe that often gets overlooked. I would never envision myself getting scored on, but I was aware and knew that even in my best season, I was still letting in two goals a game. I've let in thousands of goals in my career, but knowing that the game is built on mistakes, it's your preparation process that is used to help eliminate those mistakes. And not just your mistakes, but your teammates' mistakes as well. Knowing that you're ready to do whatever it takes going into a game and that you're prepared for all scenarios — whether it's getting scored on in the first minute or having a shutout ruined in the last minute — that is always the key."

Goldman: Was there ever a time where you struggled with this aspect of your game?

Turco: "I had a hard time with that in college because I was on a good team, was not seeing much action, and would be letting in goals that I should've had. Nobody really noticed because we were winning these games, but I really had to teach myself to get over that mental hurdle. When I was younger, it was really tough mentally to stay in the game and not let my mind wander for long periods of time. But I started to develop the skill on my own by breaking the game down into smaller five-minute stages like Tony Esposito would do, or I would try to continually watch the play in the other end. I would skate to the boards between whistles and only went one way every time, and I would rarely screw that up. The reason for doing these things was because when it was time not to think, I was in the now. But when it came time to think about what was going on, I was being forced to not think, so my goal was to put everything I had into making sure I was in the right position and just reacting. Based on my experiences, I wasn't thinking about anything else, I was just letting plays come to me and therefore I wasn't agitated or preoccupied or linear with my focus. I was very open and receptive to all the little signs, and all the while, being able to react to the puck. That was only attainable because of the mental preparation and the work that went into it."

Goldman: How exactly did you learn to correctly prepare your mind in order to attain the level of clear focus you needed to be at your best?

Turco: "Earlier in my career, things went so well for me that I really thought I was pretty invincible, and I almost felt like nothing could happen to me. I wasn't stopping every puck, but knowing what I wanted to accomplish, having those goals and meeting those goals routinely because of the focus and dedication I had, I knew I was doing the right things. It got to the point where I never thought I could screw up. But when I was getting paid to win, there were times when I did lose sight of my job. In my mind, living up to the contract became more important than stopping the puck. Being the best I could be got to the point that it was transcending the things I needed to do to play the position the way I needed to play it. But I also appreciated that sometimes I was more concerned about my teammates and what they were doing, or what was going on off the ice. Having to put that away and almost not care about those things was hard and it hurt me, because that was my human nature and that's just who I was. I am a caring person and that aspect of it was affecting my game. Even after a while, and even when I was working with a mental skills coach and a sports psychologist, because of my caring attitude, everything I would think of during a game wouldn't allow me to turn off my brain and just read and react and play my best. I was so concerned with off-ice stuff, or getting scored on, or what I'd say to reporters and others, or what excuses I could make up to feel better, that in my brain, I was just thinking about way too many things. What I had to learn to do – and it took me years to learn it – was to appreciate the thoughts that I had when I was playing. Anything under the sun that you could imagine, it was going through my head. But what I eventually realized was that a majority of my thoughts were well-deserved, well-intentioned, and were ultimately caring thoughts. At that point, my preparation finally improved because I just learned to appreciate them. I'd allow myself to finish the thought that I was having, and then I would forget it. I'd appreciate that each individual thought had value in my life, but I'd quickly realize it wasn't helping me accomplish my goal of playing in the now. So that whole process helped me get back to what I should've been doing within games."

Goldman: Once you figured out that aspect of your mental preparation, was there ever a time where you struggled with your identity as a goalie?

Turco: "No, because you could never say that Marty Turco was 'this type' of goalie. I might be this type today, but I might change things to become this other type of goalie in the future. We all evolve, our brains evolve, our nerve endings change, and our impulses change. We have an innate ability, both physically and mentally, to train our bodies and minds and ultimately change who we are. So we're always a work in progress, and that's why I think my success as an elite goalie always reverted back to preparation. You have to be understanding of what pitfalls may be ahead, what it takes to win, and how to eliminate the external distractions. For example, every day in practice, something might bother you. But the biggest disturbance to being able to mentally prepare and clear your mind is carrying that something around, not talking about it, not handling it. That will really cloud your reaction time because these things are lingering in your brain. That's what every goalie is trying to do – just going out and playing. But the older you get, the harder it is to accomplish, because so many things are going on in your life."

Goldman: I want to go back to something you mentioned earlier about how you appreciate the thoughts that go through your mind, whether they are positive or negative. I wrote a chapter in this book about the importance of realizing that you will be wrong and make mistakes. We all strive for perfection, but rarely is it attainable for very long. What are your thoughts on how the influence of being right or wrong affected your mental game?

Turco: "I think one of the best things I did when I was younger was that I never tried to emulate one goaltender. I would take the best parts of the guys that I liked and the best of what they did that I thought I could do. As I got closer to the NHL, I realized that I always knew I would need to make changes, I always knew I had more to give, and I always knew that I could be better, even after my best seasons or after the years where I went deep in the playoffs. So even if you think you've played the best game ever, well, part of the goal for an elite goalie is to do that every night. So the ultimate goal comes down to preparation and understanding that you need to be in a calm state of mind away from the rink, which helps you narrow your focus into, 'alright, how can I be at my best tonight?' I certainly knew that mistakes would be made and bad times were ahead, but I made it my goal to eliminate as many of them as possible. And trust me, I've given up plenty of bad goals and made many mistakes. I gave up plenty of goals where I was 60 feet out of the net and plenty of goals from some of the worst players imaginable, and it's a bad, lonely feeling. But what makes or breaks guys at the highest levels is when they can't get over it. For me, it was an adjustment to get over bad goals or to play great after allowing a bad goal. That's why I didn't take time off in practices. When I was practicing, I had to perform like it was a game. To me, it just all comes back to preparation. Even the best in the world have had some horrible experiences that the general public would likely never get over, never come out from beneath that rock for a long time. But knowing that you can accept the mistake or that you were guessing or doing something wrong, well, then you know you can stop it the next time. Then it's just making sure that you do, and then it becomes a matter of executing. Anything can happen, but you're only at your best when you're living in the exact moment that you're in. It's just you and the game. No matter what it is that is bothering you, it's totally irrelevant to what you're doing in the now. It doesn't matter if you made the best save of your life against the best player in the world five minutes ago, because it is completely meaningless and has nothing to do with the N-O-W. Over my career, I developed different types of scenarios like this with word choices like 'now' and other phrases I'd say as guys were coming down the ice, just to narrow my focus on playing in the moment."

Goldman: We've learned through lessons in this book that getting in the zone is usually attained by playing in the moment. How do you explain what it's like to get in the zone during games?

Turco: "It's hard to summon it, but you can be in the zone without knowing it. You always want to get there and you can always work on different stimuli that can help you get there. But if you're always believing in what you're doing, even after a mistake, knowing that the belief you have is that you care and you can get better, and then you do something about it, then you are going to find a way to get back into the zone. If you're not getting better, you're getting worse."

Goldman: What if a goalie has the right intentions, is preparing with a clear mind, but is still not getting the results? What advice do you have for goalies then?

Turco: "Even though you're in a rut, you can still work at it. If you're doing the right things and coming up with a good game plan and having good practice habits, you're going to get out of it sooner than you think. Sometimes in the games that I felt the best, or felt like I played really well, I'd watch my saves afterwards and realize I wasn't as good as I thought I was, or got really lucky on a few. The point to that is this: the highs aren't as high as you think, and the lows aren't as low as you think. Even in your darkest moments, you need to get back out there and work on solidifying strong work habits that will last you a lifetime. You can develop the work ethic and good habits, but you still need to reinforce them on a consistent basis. That sounds very physical or technical, but at the end of the day, it all falls under your mental capacity. That was one of the things I was most proud of in my career; it was my ability to look ahead, plan it, and always play in the now. As I'm speaking to you, I'm going through a lot of situations where this lesson was learned and most of these memories stem from practice. That's where you have to learn to be good and push yourself to be the best and fight for every puck."

Goldman: I wanted to ask you about a topic that we discussed in another chapter. For being an elite goalie with an All-Star profile, how important was it for you to stay humble with your approach and identity? I think pride gets in the way of a lot of young goalies and they develop an inflated ego, especially with today's obsession with social media. Can you talk about that experience in your career?

Turco: "I'll start by saying that goaltenders are supposed to be confident. You often hear the line that goalies should walk the fine line between being confident and cocky, but without going overboard. Appreciate moments where you let yourself go and show some swagger, but don't let your ego become inflated. It can become a highly detrimental influence. It looks terrible when it's your job to win but you let your ego get in the way. Having confidence while staying humble is super important, and there's a lot of documented reasons why goalies have been unable to do this and have had that problem. But to let your ego get in the way and to be arrogant, well that's pretty much like saying you're as good as you'll ever be. When you're confident, you play at your best, but you know and understand that you can still improve. You also understand that when you're humble, it's hard work to stay at that high level. Part of the reason I got paid what I did was because I stayed healthy, but also because I gave a huge crap about my teammates. In order to be humble, you have to allow yourself to bring others into your life and think about others and not let yourself get in your own way. It's a tough enough position to mentally handle, let alone thinking you're the king and expecting to be treated like a king. That's not really how it works. I have been called arrogant and cocky at times and maybe I deserved it, but maybe those people didn't really know me. I had to play confidently and that's what I needed to do to be at my best, and I believed in what I was doing, especially playing the puck the way I did. If you don't believe in what you're doing, you need to change it. But if you think you're the best, you're never going to change for the better. People and other goalies will start to pass you by, and even worse, nobody will want to be around you."

Goldman: If a goalie is feeling confident but wants to stay humble, I believe body language becomes important. How would you explain the importance of body language?

Turco: "The coolest yet strangest viewpoint in sports is when a goaltender gets scored on. Whether it's in peewees or at the pros, everyone looks at you. How you handle yourself immediately after that and the mannerisms you display are so powerful in terms of the confidence of your team, how the momentum shifts will go, how you're going to play, and what the other team thinks in regards to scoring again. It's an unenviable position to be in, one that carries so much power and persuasion that it is almost unfair. I promise you, when you have a guy that routinely handles it poorly – with his arms in the air, looking around at his teammates, or blaming others for what happened and getting agitated – it will be bad. The mannerisms become so important because it's almost unteachable, and that again comes back to preparation and thinking about how you will react when you get scored on before you go play. That is the best thing for you in terms of your subconscious mentality because you can't tell your body how to move or twitch unless it's already happening. Positive body language has to happen naturally, but if you can appreciate it and remain humble and have confidence that you won't make the mistake again with a positive attitude and outlook, then I think that's where you can really shine and really relish the position. That's what body language can do – it can transcend and transform a whole team. If you want to grow and move on and be at your ultimate best, you have to take care of your body language. It can be agitating at times when you're giving up weak goals, but the ones that handle those situations the best are the ones that end up being the best."

Goldman: What was the most difficult stage of your career? Was there a time where you may have felt completely helpless or desolate, like there was no way out? How did you handle that and how did you ultimately get over that obstacle?

Turco: "There's two things that I would say. One was during my sophomore year in college. We lost in triple OT and played well, but didn't win. I started my sophomore year and maybe I was cocky or maybe didn't appreciate the opportunity and I don't think I worked very hard that summer. We had a great team but I was letting in goals that got lost in the shuffle. We went to my hometown to play a team in college and they were good. I didn't play great and lost a couple of big games. My coach had a heart-to-heart with me afterwards and kind of pointed his finger and asked for me to be better and was questioning things I was doing on and off the ice, and more importantly, what I wasn't doing. He was a great coach, but I had a hard time with that and I didn't handle it particularly well. So what I had to do was talk about it with other people, and then remind myself that I was going to be able to work through it. Nothing replaces work. Even though you may not feel better the next day or the next week, if you work hard to do the right things, then eventually you'll get it straightened out. The second one was a hard time in the middle of my NHL career after we lost to the Avalanche in the first round of the playoffs two seasons in a row. I was one of the bigger guys on the Stars and was talking to reporters on a daily basis. It got to the point where I was answering made up questions in my head and coming up with excuses for something I had done during the freaking game. It went on for a long time and it really, really hindered my play, and I don't think I understood why at the time. I didn't have a regular goalie coach and I was kind of on my own. That was a tough time for me and I got caught in a rut. But once again, I just had to talk to someone and stop making excuses for myself. I realized that instead of waiting for someone else to do something for me, I was just going to worry about myself. I had a hard time being selfish and I was worried about my teammates and what others thought, so I had to learn to be selfish, which was a tough one."

Goldman: Everyone we spoke to in this book has mentioned how important it was to have support along the way to becoming an elite goalie. Can you talk a little bit about the support you've had in your career?

Turco: "I don't know if I believe in Karma, but I've probably been the most fortunate guy to have the support I've had. I've known my wife since high school and we went through the whole thing together, from being poor college kids to making 50 grand in the minors and having a great time. So I'll say this — my coaches, my teammates — I always loved them. But after our second time losing against the Avalanche in the first round, as a goalie, you take a lot of heat losing a series in five games. After the season ended in Game 5, my general manager was Doug Armstrong and he was sitting there. He was upset and I was bummed out dragging my ass back to the bus. He waited around and came up to me specifically and looked at me and said, 'Hey Marty, I believe in you. I believe in you as a goaltender, and you just keep working at it and we'll get these other guys on board.' When he saw me at my lowest as a professional and knowing that he paid me to win, for him to come over and say that was huge and something that I'll never forget."

Goldman: In closing, how did that affect you going forward? Was there anything that resonated with you today besides the actual memory?

Turco: "It just reminded me that even though things on the outside looked a certain way, I still had the belief that I was doing things the right way and was training the right way. So I think instead of changing just for the sake of changing things after a tough series, I just kept going down the same path. He reminded me that I was on the right path and that I was doing the right things, and that made me believe in myself."

Chapter 6
LETTING GO OF YOUR EGO

"True humility is not thinking less of yourself; it is thinking of yourself less."
—C.S. Lewis

Throughout this book, you will read different passages from elite goalies that reference the importance of being humble. We asked for their thoughts on the topic of humility because it is intimately and intrinsically tied to one of the most important lessons on becoming an elite goaltender – egolessness.

Most of you already have a basic understanding of the term Ego. For goalies, having an ego means you have an inflated or unrealistic sense of self-worth. For lack of a better term, you think you're God's gift to goaltending, the best goalie known to man, and therefore nobody else should try giving you advice, feedback, or teaching points on how to improve. Having an inflated ego also means you place an unhealthy or excessive emphasis on how you look and act in public, or when other people are watching you play.

We're willing to venture you have probably met or known a hockey player with a big ego, so think about how they acted for a moment. Did they come off a little fake, a little too materialistic, or maybe even obnoxiously self-centered? Did they spend excessive amounts of time talking about their own accolades and accomplishments, yet rarely asked anyone else about their background or past? If they asked you anything at all, was it what you thought of them? And during the moments when you happened to be talking about someone or something besides them, did you notice that they weren't even really paying attention to what you were actually saying?

Goalies with big egos see themselves as the center of their universe. They consider themselves infallible, all-knowing, or as flawless performers. Even in losses and blatantly weak performances, a goalie with a big ego makes excuses after a mistake, deflecting blame or fault away from themselves and onto anyone or anything else. They exhibit poor or negative body language by rolling their eyes, slamming their stick on the ice, or by giving the icy death stare to their defensemen. You know the signs, because at some point in time, you may have also done these things, possibly without even knowing it.

Elite goalie coaches and scouts will quickly tell you that goalies with excessive pride and inflated egos almost always finish last. That's because these goalies rarely have the skills and success to back up their sense of pride. If the goalie can't back up those skills and handle those higher expectations, they are likely to be downgraded compared to a goalie with lesser skill but an egoless attitude.

As you can imagine, excessive pride and an inflated ego are massive roadblocks on the path to becoming an elite goaltender.

Since the size of your ego is constantly in a state of flux depending on your situation and emotions, the lesson for you as the student is to learn how to remove that roadblock from ever existing. You learn this by first understanding why your ego's reflection (i.e., the way other people perceive your ego) is so important to manage, and then by learning how to play without an ego. Finally, you must learn to keep it balanced as you continue to evolve and develop.

The ability to moderate and manage one's ego does not happen overnight. Just like you have heard many times in this book, the ultimate weapon in this particular lesson is experience and self-reflection.

But there's no better time or place to start than right here, right now. And while we're more than happy to help you with the first two parts, you're on your own for the third.

*Author's Note: Both Marty Turco and Chris Mason discuss humility and the power of body language in their interviews, so be sure to read their insights if you haven't already.

You often hear head coaches say they want their goalies to be "borderline cocky" or to have that perfect balance between confidence and cockiness. This is true – you should carry yourself with a certain sense of pride and you should exhibit body language that reflects an intimidating, confident goalie with some swagger. But you must also realize that, while displaying perseverance and toughness in all facets of the game is a good thing, you must exhibit situational awareness and know when your attitude becomes excessive. You must be careful and conscientious of how you react when things go right and wrong, because people are watching. How you act in all of these moments can significantly alter the mood and emotions of everyone around you, as well as how they perceive your character.

Consider how your identity, attitude, and character reflect upon others. How do you carry yourself in practices? How do you communicate with your teammates in the locker room? How much time do you spend showing off your gear, your stats, and your swag on social media platforms like Facebook and Twitter? How much merit do you place on the number of friends or followers you have? How much energy do you put into managing your style and what you look like in public? How much time do you spend thinking about what others think of you?

Be honest with yourself in this moment of reflection.

If you think you invest a lot of time and importance on your image, don't get down on yourself. Every pro athlete and every human being has experienced an inflated ego at some point in time. It's nearly impossible to avoid an inflated ego at times, because it is a part of the human condition. We all experience moments when we enjoy showing off our accolades or place great importance on how we look. It's inescapable in today's society, because first impressions are key; they do mean a lot. It's only normal to want to "look good, feel good, play good."

That is fine and understandable. Particularly, considering the goalie is "on an island" and the only one with custom equipment that reflects an individual style and personality, there will always be a certain sense of ego being reflected to others. You also know that you can't control what others think of you or how they think of you, and this is why your sense of worth and your sense of identity in the eyes of others becomes a consuming, chaotic thought in your mind. This answers the first question: Why it is so important to manage the ego when developing and playing the position? The more you're thinking about what others think of you, the less you're playing in the moment with a clear mind.

The next question to answer is why, and how, to play without an ego. Part of this answer is simple: because your body language is capable of reflecting the mental and emotional state of the entire team. When the puck enters the crease, all eyes are on you in that single moment. And since everyone is connected in that single moment, how you act wields the unbelievable power to alter the mood, change the momentum, and influence the emotions and beliefs of everyone connected to that moment's outcome. Everyone will have a belief and a thought and an opinion on what you do in that moment.

The same goes for your actions and reactions in a myriad of other moments. Are you laughing on the bench at the wrong times? Are you goofing off during practice when scouts are in the stands? Do you fail to focus on what your coach is saying when he's giving a pre-game speech?

Regardless of the situation, you must realize that whether you succeed or fail in certain moments, and regardless of where the faults lie, you are responsible for your actions and reactions. That is what you can control, and that is what you must manage.

This is why it is absolutely vital for developing goaltenders to try and achieve a state of mind where they stay positive whether things go right or wrong. While it's not an easy thing to do, by always maintaining positive body language and emotional stability when all eyes are on you, you escape the perils of over-thinking or worrying about your own self-identity. Focus on the next play, keep your eyes and body and response mechanisms calm, try to smile, replay the situation in your mind, analyze, adjust, and move forward.

You should also remember to take failures the same way you take successes.

In order to play without an ego, everything you do should also be for the good of the team. Do the little things that prove you care more about your teammates than yourself – they go a long way. Examples of this could be taking shots after practice, praising one teammate's accomplishments, goals, or blocked shots at least once a day, keeping negative opinions on players to yourself. Care not what your teammates think of your skills, but rather what your skills can bring to make the team better.

All of these things reflect a single emotional trait that incorporates all three pillars of elite goaltending, which allows you to drop the ego when the moment matters – Humility.

Being humble does not necessarily mean you have to break yourself down or look at yourself in a negative light. Instead, it simply means that you should not really think about yourself at all. The more thoughts in your mind, the more noise you create. Conversely, the less you're thinking, the easier it is to play "in the moment" with a clear mind.

You are who you are – be comfortable and happy in your own skin and in your own mind.

Humble goaltenders are freed from the chains of their egos because they are secure. They accept the fact that they are merely one piece of their team's success, that they are small creatures in the infinitely large world around them, and that they are not in control of a lot of things that transpire in a game. They recognize they are vulnerable to bad bounces, bad calls from the referee, or certain decisions made by their head coach.

A humble goaltender also realizes something we explained in the chapter regarding the role of the spirit – their skills and gifts were given to them by something more powerful than themselves. Once that realization lays a foundation in your own mental approach, when you do mess up, your humility keeps you from having to cover up or hide those faults. Instead, you forgive, learn from it, forget it, and move on in an even-keeled manner. Mistakes no longer surprise, anger, or scare you because you realize your fallibility is a part of being human.

The bottom line is that a humble goaltender is in touch with the realities of playing a position that is sometimes impacted by factors you cannot control. Therefore, the true balance of managing your ego comes from saying, "Win or lose, I am an athlete gaining experience. I am still human and I will make mistakes."

*Author's Note: Here we direct you to the chapter on "Why Being Wrong is Right." By professing to the world around us that we are capable of being wrong, we reflect a more humble character.

Similar to the Three Pillars of Elite Goaltending, you can visualize a balanced ego as three interconnected parts: Humility supports clarity, clarity supports thoughtlessness, and thoughtlessness establishes balance, due to the ability to play and live in the moment.

Humility also means you really have nothing to prove to anyone around you, because you have no urge to flaunt your strengths or your skills. Humility leads to meekness, but meekness is not a weakness. It is strength under control – a certain type of power used to boost the morale and momentum of your team, not tear down the insecurities of others.

An all-encompassing way to balance and manage the ego is by striving to be a selfless person. Humble goalies are great leaders and listeners; they are genuinely interested and delighted in what others have to say. By doing this, goalies make those around them feel special and worthy as a teammate.

The teaching points above are the keys to remember as you work toward balancing your ego. Let go of your ego by acting like nothing is about you specifically, but rather a reflection of your part of the team's journey. Take genuine joy in helping others who have helped you, and always support your teammates.

Think back to all the interviews you've seen from NHL goaltenders on television. Do you notice how they always deflect praise after a shutout and discuss how well their defensemen played, how well they pushed shots to the corners, and how well they played as a team? This is one of the ultimate forms of a goalie managing their ego in the public eye. They think and speak in the plural form (we, they) instead of the singular or possessive form (I, me). They take praise with thanks, yet reflect that praise right back to those who helped them achieve success.

When shallowness and beauty is all that consumes your mind and body, your true spirit is thrust to the bottom. This causes you to lose the sense of who you really are. People no longer want to be around you and your mind becomes clouded with insignificant thoughts that pull you further away from your true goal of becoming an elite goaltender.

Not only will a balanced ego improve your own attitude and personality, but it will clear your mind of unnecessary thoughts and allow you to play peacefully.

-Goldman

Chapter 7
THE FIT MIND

"The consciousness of self is the greatest hindrance to the proper execution of all physical action."—Bruce Lee

After reading the first six chapters of this book, you should now have a much better understanding of the Three Pillars of Elite Goaltending and the importance of the connection between the body, mind, and spirit.

As special athletes that face a very unique set of mental and technical challenges, goalies must overcome physical obstacles that require the use of mental prowess to complete a shutout, win a game, or even make it through a difficult practice. The feeling of accomplishment we enjoy and experience when we know we used our minds to propel our physical bodies is one of the ultimate highs of being a goaltender. It does not come easy, and as a result, we walk away with great inner pride.

In addition, we know that our physical bodies only grow when we are at rest. Muscle mass increases as we sleep, while a true indicator of cardiovascular health is how quickly our heart rates return to normal after a burst of energy. When we finish a workout or when a game ends, we know it is time to rest. And we are naturally very good at resting our bodies.

However, many of us have trouble resting our minds. The brain is arguably the strongest muscle in the body. It is the control center for physical, mental, and emotional activity. So even when we sleep, our brains are active, controlling our breathing, regulating our hearts, and dreaming. In fact, our brains are active every moment of our lives, yet unlike our bodies, our minds rarely get the rest they need and deserve.

Strengthening the mind can lead to amazing changes, but how do we give the mind the rest it needs in order to grow?

The answer lies in Meditation.

Meditation is learning how to harness the power of the mind by using the absence of thought to create an abundance of power. Successful meditation can give us the same feeling of accomplishment that results from the completion of a strenuous physical workout. We just have to learn how to do it and commit ourselves to staying the course.

Like anything else regarding the development of a new skill, proper meditation takes practice, and many of us give up before we have even given ourselves a chance. The most important thing to remember when beginning anything new is to be kind to yourself. Give yourself the time and space you need to become skilled at quieting your mind.

At the start, it may be easier for you to do this while running, biking, or listening to music. That is fine. Do whatever it takes for you to begin to enter a mindset where you are not actively engaging your brain in any type of thought.

But more importantly, do it often. Build it into your daily routine, make it a regular occurrence. As you begin to relax, let go of the tendency to actively think and problem solve your way through life's various situations. Just breathe. Fall into a rhythm and let life flow in the moment.

By creating this simple escape from reality on a regular basis, you will find your reality shifting. As time passes, you will find yourself in a better place than before. You will strengthen your mind the way you strengthen your muscles – by giving it the rest it so greatly deserves.

-Valley

Chapter 8
TALKING WITH CHRIS MASON

Author's Note: The following interview with former Nashville Predators, St. Louis Blues, and Winnipeg Jets goaltender Chris Mason took place during the NHL lockout in the winter of 2012. He's an excellent addition to our collection of interviews because of his vast experience. Over his 317-game NHL career, Mason played a myriad of different roles on different types of teams, so he's seen a little bit of everything. As a result, he brings a wealth of knowledge on the mental game. He is currently playing for Ritten-Renon in the Italian Elite League.

Goldman: For an esteemed veteran like yourself, I'd love just a brief background on how you first became a goalie.

Mason: "Well, especially at my age, I think everyone that is from Canada wants to play hockey at a young age. I happened to start when I was six years old. I started playing out as a forward, but when I was growing up, teams would give every player a chance to be the goalie. I always enjoyed putting on the goalie equipment and being in that position, so I continued down that path until Atoms, when I had to decide to go one way or the other…and I continued to get my turn in the net. The biggest thing for me was that I was a pretty good hockey player, but I was always really drawn to the equipment and the position, so I always enjoyed playing it when I had the chance. But it wasn't until I decided to go to Andy Moog's goalie school when I was 11 years old – he was my favorite goalie at the time, so that was pretty special for me – that I finally made up my mind. I've been a goalie ever since."

Goldman: Do you think the competitive drive to be the best and to win every game was always a part of your mental makeup, or do you feel like it came a little later after being in net for a few years?

Mason: "I remember my first year playing the game, when I had never even been on skates before. My parents took me to some type of tryout, but I couldn't skate, so my mom was crying in the stands because they felt bad and kind of embarrassed for me. They tell me the story that I got in the car after the tryout and said that I knew they spent a lot of money on buying the equipment, but told them I would stick it out and keep playing. So at first I wasn't very good at all, and I didn't really have that drive to be the best. But the next year I was one of the top players in my age group in the surrounding programs. Once I got good, I had that competitive drive for sure. I think it was always in me, it just took a while for it to come out."

Goldman: Is there any specific moment in time where you gained a lot of confidence, or something specific that happened that kind of fueled you to want to play at a higher level?

Mason: "I think that happened once they started doing regular tryouts, and then I started competing and trying out against different goalies. When you're growing up, the goalie that's a year older than you, you try to measure up to them. For me, goaltending-wise, it was when I started playing the travel teams and teams from other cities. I guess hockey started to become a bigger deal at that time, and along with that goes the coaching and the competitive nature of the games you're playing in as well."

Goldman: Besides Andy Moog, was there anyone that was really influential to you as a kid that showed you that you were capable of being an elite goalie?

Mason: "For me, I just loved all goalies. I would draw them and design goalie masks and get hockey cards and then draw every goalie, starting with guys like Mike Palmateer and other goalies in that era. I also remember when Eddy Belfour first came into the league. Everybody loved the Eagle on his mask and his style of play was a little different than everyone else's at the time. When I played street hockey growing up, I remember I would be Felix Potvin or Belfour and then emulate their style and try to do the things they were doing. I just loved that, especially when I grew up, because every goalie was so much different back then. I think now there are still a lot of differences, but a lot of the training is becoming more similar and so there are a lot of guys on a larger scale training the same way. But I just remember watching guys back then, and every goalie was so different from the next, so it was pretty fun growing up watching goalies that way and learning how to play the position. So I don't think I could single out one or two guys because I loved all of them, and I especially loved their equipment and the way they played. I just loved watching them all."

Goldman: Do you think it was important that you had those influences, and that the goalies you were watching back then were so different in terms of how you developed your game?

Mason: "Yeah, for sure. I went to a couple of hockey schools in the summer when I was growing up, but when I think about it now, I just feel very fortunate that I've had such good influences during my youth years, and more recently, good goalie coaching as a professional. They've all helped me evolve since the position has evolved so much lately. The technique and the way guys train and do video breakdowns is unbelievable. For me growing up, I felt like you just went in there and kind of used your own athleticism and you tried to basically stop the puck any way you could because there wasn't as much specialized training as there is today. I didn't have a true goalie coach until I turned pro, so I was basically just sitting there until I was 21 years old and was lucky enough to meet Mitch Korn. My first pro goalie coach was actually Francois Allaire when I played in Cincinnati, and that was when the blocking and the Quebec goalies had gotten into the bigger equipment. That was totally out of my comfort zone because I wore smaller equipment and tried to rely on my athleticism and seeing the puck, so it wasn't very fancy, but it got the job done for me at that point. Then I got traded to Nashville and met Mitch and he really, really helped me have a greater understanding of the position. That's when I started to realize how much detail and thought was put into it. I was fortunate enough to work with him for almost 10 years between Milwaukee and Nashville."

Goldman: Knowing that the position is so refined these days and goalies are doing so much video breakdown, how important is it to still be able to rely on your natural athleticism? You focus so hard in practice

on the technical side, but at the end of the day, when the puck drops for a game, you have to rely on those instincts.

Mason: "Yeah, I totally agree. I've skated a bunch in the summers with kids that are still in the minor league hockey system. You do skating drills with some of these kids, and I'm really blown away at how well they can move and skate in there, and how strong they are on their feet, and how they are moving around when they are already down. When you're doing drills and you know when the shots are coming and where they are coming from and it's kind of a set A-to-B in a formation, they look really good. But I find that once you start giving the shooters more freedom, a lot of kids get so locked in that it's almost a little robotic, and almost on autopilot in a way. I think that's coming out more because guys are starting to say you need to be a bit looser with your hands and they have to be free so you can move and follow the puck instead of getting locked in. The higher level you get to, the guys don't need a lot of room to score. The way it was with all the technical training in the last 10 years, it was really being forgotten about how to scramble, or how to use natural ability to make a save when you're totally out of it, or how you contort your body in some way just to get something on the puck. I think a lot of guys are starting to realize it now that just using the technical side isn't always the best way of going about it."

Goldman: How do you personally balance that dynamic? How do you train so hard every day and go through the drills and really focus on angles and positioning, but then switch that off and just play in the moment when the game starts?

Mason: "For me, that's when practice is such an invaluable tool. In my career, most of it has been as a backup, so practices have become even more important for a guy like me, someone who doesn't play as much. When you're playing all the time, the bottom line is that you've got to get it done, so you do have the opportunity to work on stuff. But for me, I need to do it over and over again, and my movements need to become second nature. A lot of this stuff and the way I play now, I've learned and developed that into my style of play in practice. It takes me more time than a younger guy. So things like the VH-stance on the side of the net, well that has never been comfortable for me, and I've tried to do it over and over, and I just don't feel comfortable because I feel locked in, and it's just not a good position for me. I've gotten better at it, and I use it more on my blocker side than my glove side, but that's something I'm still trying to work on in practice. For me, the big thing has been the communication with my goalie coaches, letting them know what I need to work on. They're so good at teaching it, and that's a whole different skill set. And I've been fortunate to have worked with some great coaches that have just helped me so much to stay in the league, so I'm really fortunate that way, and I wouldn't be in the league this long if it wasn't for them."

Goldman: Reflecting back on your career and knowing the steps you've had to take whether it was with Nashville or St. Louis or Winnipeg, talk a little about how you handled the day-to-day pressure mentally knowing you had these opportunities and wanted to make the most of it?

Mason: "When I got my first real shot to be a starter in Nashville, they traded Tomas Vokoun and didn't sign a bunch of guys like Paul Kariya, Scott Hartnell, and Kimmo Timonen. I remember I got a shutout in my first game, and let in just one goal in my second game, so I was off to a great start. But things didn't go so well after that, and I put so much pressure on myself to perform that there were a lot more mental ups and downs for me that year. It was a huge adjustment, and it was a tough situation with our team. A lot of guys were trying to find their identity, myself included, and how to handle the situation. We had Dan Ellis come in after making the team in camp and he ended up played amazing that year, so took the job over for me in the second half of the season. So that was also tough, but again, it was one of those things that helped me prepare for my next opportunity, which was in St. Louis. Manny Legace and I were playing together until he got hurt, and I played well when that happened, so I took that job over and I played the last 33 or 34 games in a row. You just get into that position where you had the experience before, and so I felt more equipped to handle it. You get in that comfort zone and you feel good, and if I had a bad game I was able to shake it off quicker because I knew I was playing the next game, so it all seemed to fall into place in St. Louis."

Goldman: Can you talk a little more about that comfort zone in St. Louis, and how knowing what your situation was allowed you to be more mentally stable. How did that help you perform at a more consistent level?

Mason: "Knowing you are the guy does help because it takes the uncertainty out of the equation. But having said that, I've been in situations where I know I wasn't the guy, then you have that competition, and I think that's healthy too. It's just a little different because your schedule isn't set in stone and you might not know exactly when you're going to play next, so you have those things to worry about. It makes the preparation that you go through to play that much more important, because you don't know when you're going to use it. When I was in St. Louis, it just almost seemed like everything slowed down. I read plays better, I found the pucks through traffic, and I was able to anticipate better. You just create more time for yourself by being more efficient in your movements because you're not over-doing things. I was such an intense guy back then, so I've learned to harness it and use in a positive way, instead of trying so hard to make all these big saves all the time. When that happens, I have to work so hard to get back up, so it almost feels like you're going out and attacking the puck. When I'm at my best, I'm standing there and I'm calm and I'm letting things come to me. I'm letting the game happen, and reacting accordingly. Not in a physical sense, but more in a mental sense. When you see guys playing well, you know they're just letting things happen and reacting."

Goldman: You're in a different stage in your career now with your second stint in Nashville. So how do you get yourself into that same mindset now that you're not playing on a nightly basis anymore?

Mason: "Well for me, I actually had the fortune of being in both positions. I've never been in a major backup role, but I'd have times where I wouldn't play much but I'd get to play in the minors. My first year in the NHL, I played behind Vokoun and he was a workhorse. I knew I wasn't going to play a lot, but I knew if I didn't play well, I wouldn't be in the NHL. So I had to change the way I practiced. The way I prepared for games I knew I wasn't playing, well I prepared the same way as if I was playing, so that if I did have to play, it wouldn't be awkward. So I would continue to do my routine and prepare each day as if I was playing. I remember my first few NHL games, and how I thought making the NHL was the greatest accomplishment, and how it was so much bigger than I could have imagined. I remember Mitch saying I was playing pretty good at the time, but I needed to get a win here pretty soon. My first win was against Colorado and I wasn't even supposed to play that night, and I got to play. I remember being so nervous before that game, and once the game started, because I had been preparing and calming my nerves, I was able to go out there and just let things happen, and the result was very positive."

Goldman: When you talk about preparing and you have that routine, are there are one or two things that you do specifically that gets you into that relaxed and ready state of mind?

Mason: "There's definitely physical things I do to get my body warm and stretched and things like that. I have routines that I adjust to meetings and stuff like that. But probably about 45 minutes before warm-up, I'll just sit in my stall and I'll go through this visual routine of seeing pucks coming off left-handed and right-handed shooters, or guys just shooting over my shoulders, and I'll visualize how it looks coming off a stick. I'll also visualize tracking pucks as they pass pucks across my body. I go through a visual routine like that every time I play, and like I said, I do it now when I'm not playing because you never know. A lot of the teams I've played on, you're in the playoff race and there are so many points that every game is crucial. So as a backup goalie, you have an opportunity to make a difference because the games you're playing are the same value as the others, just not as frequent. A lot of it also starts the night before, like making sure I consume the kind of things I can eat that won't upset my stomach, and stuff like that. That's something I've developed over time."

Goldman: I know that every NHL goalie has the ability to self-visualize. A lot of goalies I talk to, even when they were young, had those dreams of winning the Stanley Cup. Can you talk about the discipline it takes to utilize visualization as a solid mental tool on a daily basis?

Mason: "I really think it is so important to self-visualize. I think a lot of it too is knowing how to do it for your opponent's tendencies. It really gives you a valuable tool to use during and before games because when you visualize things, and you've watched video, and you can see them setting up plays and preparing for what you're going to do, it often happens in the game, and that helps you. In the back of your mind you've been there a little bit, and you feel a little more prepared for those situations."

Goldman: What kind of things do you work on right now in terms of where you are in your career? Mitch likes to call you a "low-maintenance" goalie, so what is it that makes you so solid in your routine?

Mason: "I think at this point it does, but if I were to look back at my career, I'm proud of my work ethic. I always wanted to get better and I was willing to do anything and listen to anybody, and I was willing to learn and try everything. I just wanted to stay in the NHL and get better. Mitch helped me a great deal, as did Rick Wamsley and Clint Malarchuk. All these guys helped me, and my willingness to listen and to learn and to get better is probably the thing I'm most proud of. To be a low-maintenance guy is important because I never ever wanted to be a pain in the butt, or to be the guy that was second-guessing their direction or guidance. I was just always ready to compete and do whatever it took. I knew I wasn't playing, so I'd work my butt off to try and help my teammates get better, by bringing that intensity, mainly so that they're shooting on a backup who is trying to stop everything. To be at this point in my career, I look forward to whatever happens next and I'm proud of the reputation I've developed. For Mitch to say I'm a low-maintenance guy, that's a compliment. I'm capable of fulfilling the niche of having to play 10 or 15 or 20 games, I've been in all situations before, so that makes the transition to come back easier for me and for them."

Goldman: I notice today with a lot of younger goalies that they have egos, and it doesn't distract them from being focused or mentally prepared. Can you talk about the importance of not letting your ego get in the way?

Mason: "I don't think anyone really likes a guy with an ego. To me, it's an act, and that's not natural. In my opinion, it's an insecurity when you have to outwardly act like someone you're not, or when you have an unauthentic personality. It's tough for the guys with egos, because a lot of times they're not viewed as good teammates because they're so focused on their own image and how they're viewed by other people and fans. I've never been a fan of that outward cockiness or arrogance, but I guess it does work for some guys, because it gives them an edge. But personally I'm not a big fan of that. It's tough to get away with it in a dressing room because most guys just call you out. When I was younger, I couldn't even imagine barely stating my own opinion, but it's changed a little bit over the years."

Goldman: I think it's so important for goalies today to realize you have to be a team player, and do whatever it takes to help your team win. You have to look good and feel good to play good, but sometimes I feel like younger goalies are more concerned with how they look, and who is watching them, as opposed to doing whatever they can to stop the puck. Mike and I thought you were a great guy to talk to about this topic because you love the gear and the style so much, but you are known for having a team-first mentality. We think it's good for goalies to hear it from an NHL guy on how important it is to just go out there and be a team player first.

Mason: "That's one thing that I've know I've always had. You're playing an individual position on a team sport, and you're the only one on the ice playing goal for your team. But in a team environment, the thing that has been the most important to me is the respect. Earning the respect of my teammates is something that I work as hard as I can to earn in practice every single day. I do that partly because that's who I am, but also because I want my coaches and teammates to respect me for that. By me doing that, it says they can count on me, and that they know I have their back, even if I'm not playing. Everyone wants to play, but you have to accept the role you are given, so for me to contribute, I just make sure to work my butt off. I also make sure to be ready when I'm playing, as a form of respect to the team. I know that I've done that over my career, and that's why I'm still in the league. But like you touched on, some of it is disappearing in today's generation of goaltenders."

Goldman: I think that's the ultimate lesson and why we wanted you to be in this book. You have always had the work ethic, and you're known for being that team-first goalie. So knowing this, how did you develop that work ethic? Was it your family values?

Mason: "I think as long as I can remember, I always felt like I was just like that. My dad was like that, and he always stressed to never give up and to work hard and be the hardest working guy out there. I've definitely had influence in that department. My mom just always kind of gave me the confidence and freedom to be who I was, and taught me that it's important to don't be someone you're not. If you're a goofy bugger, that's okay too. The people that matter will accept you for who you are. I've always felt like I've had that, especially when it came to hockey. Trying to do whatever it takes to get better is the main lesson I've taken from my parents. I remember my first year in Milwaukee, goalies weren't training really hard off the ice back then. We would do some stuff, but we didn't have the type of specialized programs you see today. I had an OK year and had my end-of-the-year meetings. My strength coach said, 'you're a good kid and you work your butt off…but do you want to make the NHL?" I said yes of course, and he said I had to completely change my training regimen and get in the gym and dedicate this summer to training, because I could be in way better shape. And if I didn't, I wasn't making the NHL. I remember that big-time, and it was an eye-opener for me, especially as a goalie. It comes with the territory with hockey and being in great shape. I ended up losing 20 pounds that summer, I learned how to eat properly, I worked out harder than I ever had before, I stuck with the program, and it was one of those things where if I didn't make that change in my life, I wouldn't have made it. I'm just thankful that he pulled me aside and was completely honest with me, and I'm thankful that I listened to him."

Goldman: That's awesome, and really hammers home the lesson of work ethic. Every NHL goalie seems to learn one or two real valuable lessons that define who they are. Besides the work ethic, which sounds like it came naturally, and beyond dedicating yourself to the weight room, what's one valuable lesson that taught you the mental toughness?

Mason: "One-hundred percent, I needed the belief in myself. You have to be an honest critic. I've played with so many players that I think could've been in the NHL when I was in the minors. Guys that were more skilled than me, but they were lacking something. I just think unwavering belief in yourself is important. For whatever reason, people want to tell you that you'll never play in the NHL. Some people have heard that and it probably crushes them. For me, I've always believed I could do it. And I did whatever it took to make it."

Chapter 9
THE POWER OF WITHDRAWAL

"There are many who live in the mountains and behave as if they were in the town; they are wasting their time. It is possible to be a solitary in one's mind while living in a crowd; and it is possible for those who are solitaries to live in the crowd of their own thoughts." —*Amma Syncletica*

Over the course of this book, we have mentioned (and will continue to stress) the importance of avoiding distractions in order to achieve flow. While a "distraction" can mean different things for different goalies, an all-encompassing definition is any uncontrollable aspect of life or any mental noise that pulls you away from your ultimate goal.

While we all know we can't avoid many uncontrollable things that happen in life, as we mature, we learn how to manage this aspect of frustration within our daily lives by finding different ways to stay focused on the task at hand.

Every goalie will have his or her own methods for dealing with an uncontrollable situation, but one way to manage the chaos and frustrations that can spill negativity into our lives is to understand, and properly utilize, the power of Withdrawal.

For thousands of years, withdrawal has been practiced by spiritual figureheads in many different cultures. From early Christianity to Hinduism, Buddhism, and Judaism, extremely devoted priests, monks, athletes, warriors, and philosophers would practice what is known as Asceticism.

By removing themselves from the temptations and distractions of daily life, they ultimately became closer to themselves and their ability to achieve their true goals.

The word Asceticism is rooted in a Greek term meaning "exercise" or "training". It describes a lifestyle characterized by abstinence from various worldly pleasures, often for reasons such as becoming a stronger and more devout human being. But an ascetic abstained from certain things not because they wanted to reject life's pleasures or to be more virtuous beings, but because the process aided in their pursuit of better physical, emotional, and metaphysical health.

The etymology of the word "ascetic" is actually an adjective that refers to the physical training for athletic events. Only later did the word's usage extend to religious practices. So whether it's a warrior preparing for the battlefield, an Olympian hoping to achieve glory for their country, or today's pro goaltender preparing for the Stanley Cup Playoffs, abstaining from sex, rich foods, and other pleasures before a big competition is commonly practiced in order to mentally prepare.

In the realm of elite goaltending, as Valley explained in Chapter 7, the most common form of Asceticism is Meditation. And this is a great way to answer the question, "Why should I meditate?"

Meditation provides a wealth of benefits for goalies. Improving breathing techniques, clearing your mind, and relaxing are all excellent goals that one can achieve with a healthy dose of meditation. Additionally, meditation is a perfect way to execute the power of withdrawal because it can also help you realize just how many things can interfere with your ability to focus before a big game.

So if you're looking to achieve balance and better prepare for a game through withdrawal, ask yourself these questions:

How many times do I check my phone from the moment I get to the rink until the moment I hit the ice for a game? How much time do I spend talking to teammates and girlfriends compared to stretching and mentally preparing? How much time do I spend visualizing myself making saves, going over the opponent's roster, or discussing strategy with my defense and coaches? Do I just show up and expect success to fall in my lap, or do I execute a mental pre-game routine with a purpose?

In today's world, so many things are out there just waiting to distract you. All of these things are capable of getting in the way of how you prepare and focus and quiet your busy mind. Whether it's being on your phone, checking Twitter and Facebook, or just worrying about what people and players will say about you, it is important to know how to put on your game face, act with confidence, avoid looking for approval from others, and just be yourself.

If the act of meditating is still beyond your comfort zone, or you're slowly working your way into these previously unfamiliar methods of strengthening your mental skills, consider the many alternative forms of Withdrawal. Take a walk around the rink before you get into the locker room, or walk around a park before you head to the rink (walking meditation is a commonly used method today). Put on your headphones and listen to music in the stands before anyone else shows up. Even something as simple as riding the stationary bike before a game can help you withdraw from distractions that take place prior to a game.

Whatever it may be, try to find a few things that allow you to isolate yourself, so you can truly "tune in" to your mind and work on achieving flow before you hit the ice. Even if it's the middle of the week, or you have some down time between practice and school, little things like reading a book, writing in a journal, taking a bath, or shooting hoops by yourself can be a healthy form of non-ascetic withdrawal.

Proverbially speaking, it's harder to find yourself when you're lost among a forest full of trees. But when you stand alone on the prairie, joined only by the rolling winds, you can easily find yourself and tune into your body and your mind.

So, instead of your mind being fragmented into many different components of life, the act of Withdrawal allows you to collect your mind's energy and invest it into a singular effort – playing at your best.

Ultimately, you may wonder: How does all of this benefit you as a goaltender?

It benefits your development because it allows you to get into the rhythm of knowing and understanding the forces that can break your concentration and ruin the focus needed to play at your best. It improves your overall awareness, both mentally and metaphysically. And since our lives are filled with so much noise, different forms of Withdrawal help you find the answers you seek in the purity of silence.

Even when you are in the heat of the battle, you can find the rhythm and the flow of the game in the silence. Blocking out the noise from the crowd, closing your eyes to focus on your breathing, or repeating short mantras to yourself are methods we find elite goalies using on a game-by-game basis.

So separate yourself from the rest of the world whenever you feel pressure or anxiety or too many distractions getting in your way. Allow the silence to help you discover who you are, how you are feeling, and what you need to accomplish in order to play a relaxed, calm game. Withdraw yourself from daily life from time to time. Disconnect. Get away from it all.

For inspiration is often found in isolation.

-Goldman

Chapter 10

TALKING WITH RICHARD BACHMAN

Author's Note: The following interview with Richard Bachman took place in the Spring of 2013 during his time with the Dallas Stars. Bachman, who has worked extremely hard over the years to make it to the NHL despite being less than six feet tall, is an amazing story of perseverance and patience with the development process. For readers that may struggle with the internal battle of being a smaller goalie, this interview is for you. Bachman continues to play at the highest level imaginable for a goalie his size, as he is currently a part of the Edmonton Oilers organization.

Goldman: I guess just start by giving us a brief background on how you came to be a goaltender, and your first experience in the pads.

Bachman: "For me, I started playing hockey when I was six. I lived in a small town in upstate New York called Saranac Lake. The first year I played was basically the 1996 season, and I had just moved from Colorado to New York. It was the first season the Nordiques moved to Colorado, so I was a big fan of the Avalanche just by nature of being from Colorado. I was pretty lucky that they had Patrick Roy in there, so I had someone pretty special in net to watch while I was growing up. I played forward for a few years and everything, but for some reason, I always wanted to try goalie. I think a lot of it had to do with watching Roy and a little bit about the pads and the mask and that whole deal. So when I was about eight years old, the organization I played for actually needed a goalie for the team I played on. So they just offered if anyone wanted to try it, they covered the cost for all the pads and everything so I was just like why not. I remember the first skate getting on the ice, I mean I could barely move in those pads and stuff, but one of the first shots I took was glove side, and I caught it. So from there it kind of stuck, and that's all I've ever wanted to do is play goalie. So that's how I became a goalie. Then I would just watch any NHL games I could and I was lucky in Lake Placid because the Islanders would come out there. Garth Snow was up there signing autographs and he was a great guy so I wanted to be a goalie even more after meeting a couple of those guys and watching them play."

Goldman: Speaking of Roy, he's influenced so many goalies over his playing career. Is there anything specific that you remember about how he influenced who you are as a goalie today?

Bachman: "I think when I first started out, just being able to watch him play and idolize him, and from watching him on TV, I would kind of mimic his same moves in my living room. Sometimes I'd throw on the pads and when he'd make a save, I'd kind of do the same thing. So from that standpoint I think it helped my technique when I was younger, without even knowing it. I was actually fortunate enough when I moved back to Colorado that his son played in the same organization as me in Littleton. So I was able to meet him and work with him on the ice a few times. He was so good at teaching positioning and reading plays, and he would talk to us and show us technique, and he was all over you if your pads weren't flat on the ice and stuff. He was a little hard on you at times, but it kind of gave me that discipline to make sure I was doing everything correct from an early age. The other areas he's influenced my career is just watching him compete when they went to the Stanley Cup Finals in 1996 and then won it again in 2001. Just seeing how well he played when it mattered most was huge for me. He stepped up to the plate and threw the team on his back when they needed him the most. He wasn't perfect all the time, but he'd make one or two of those big saves that changed the momentum or kept them in the game, and you realize from seeing him do that how important it is to winning championships."

Goldman: I also had the opportunity to watch Roy as well when I was living in Colorado, and it was always his crazy focus and determination that fascinated me. Do you think that because you interacted with Roy on the ice, you have tried to reflect a lot of his same traits and mannerisms when you are playing?

Bachman: "Yeah absolutely, I think that's such a huge mindset for a goalie to have. For a while in my career, I don't know if it was superstition or not, but I almost wouldn't tell myself I was going to stop every puck. And then probably over the past five or six years, I've developed that mindset that I'm not going to be scored on. I don't think it goes so far to say that if I do get scored on that I let it affect me, but my mindset from watching him is that every shot I face, I'm going to save. I'm going to stop everything, and that's a huge part of the game, is being confident. He gives me the mindset where you don't have to be perfect all the time, but you want to be able to stop every shot in games and in practices. You don't just turn it on and off, it's a mindset you need to have every time you're on the ice."

Goldman: Dominik Hasek and Patrick Roy seem to be the two iconic goalies that were known for being as competitive in practices as they were in games. Talk a little bit about how you mentally approach practices and how it influence your game?

Bachman: "I think working hard in practice and not letting the guys score reflects on the goalie himself as a competitor, as wanting to get better, and I think the players on your team feed off that. And because of that, they have a little more confidence in you heading into a game. That's what you need - you need them to be confident in you to get the job done and when they are, they do their job a little better because they're not worried about their goalie. As far as in practices, for me, I take my warm-ups and stuff, and even then, for me, it's all about feeling the puck, but I want to stop as many as I can too. As we get going, I'll even say in my head that they're not scoring in this drill at all, and I'll kind of keep track and that will be my goal for a specific drill. That helps you not only get better and work on your technique and all that, but it really works on the mental game. Then dialing it in and focusing for that amount of time allows you to transfer it into a game."

Goldman: When you're in a practice or game, every goalie knows that it's really important to send yourself positive mental messages. How important is that to you, to keep things positive, in practice?

Bachman: "For me, practice is all about competing and not wanting to get scored on. But part of practice is that positive reinforcement where my goal is to not let them score, but at the same time, I'll tell myself 'let's be good on rebounds here,' and play messages like, 'okay, any blocker shots are going to the corners' in my mind.

That kind of stuff I think helps you become mentally stronger while making saves, but it also teaches you how to become a better goalie and work on what you need to work on in your game. So positive messages in practice is important, but I also think you need to spend some time and think a little more to get your technique down and constantly improve and sharpen those areas your game. Moving into the game, I do a number of different things where I think it actually helps me not to think too much, but it also keeps me positive and focused at the same time."

Goldman: What are some of those things?

Bachman: "A lot of it starts the night before the game. I will just visualize myself making saves and imagine how it feels. As the game gets going, basically for me, before the puck drops, I'll go through in my head and just say things like, 'alright, be on my toes, be aggressive, keep it simple, have fun, and then worry about the next shot.' So there's like five things right there I'll tell myself as the puck drops. As the play develops, all of that leaves, and then it's just focusing on that puck and how plays develop."

Goldman: Going off of what you said, can you talk a little bit about the process of having the mental and emotional patience to put in the time every day, year after year, to make it to where you are now?

Bachman: "I think trusting the process is something I've had to learn to do since I was 15 years old. Fortunately for me, it has all worked out really well, but it hasn't been easy. A lot of it is just working hard and trusting and hoping that what you're doing is the right thing. For me it kind of started when I went to prep school. I went out there and I didn't know anyone or anything, and my first year, I played probably five games. That was probably one of the hardest times in my career, just 15-16 years old, and didn't know if I wanted to go back because I didn't know if I was going to play. But I trusted what people around me were saying, that I was going to be good, and I just worked hard every day when I wasn't playing just to become better and to compete with the older guys. So I decided to go back, and it turned out for the next two years that I played almost every single game. So it worked out, but it was just trusting the process, and not getting down on myself when it didn't go how I wanted. It was almost more motivation as time went on to get out from being a backup, or motivation to get out from the ECHL in order to get into the AHL, or from out of the AHL and into the NHL. It was just about going to the rink every day and working hard and trusting that my teammates around me are doing what they need to do to help us succeed. But I also had to give them a reason to help me succeed. That was kind of my thought process going through all of the different steps right there."

Goldman: When you know that you've put in so much time and effort into trusting the process, and when you've had those situations where you get the opportunity to prove yourself, what goes through your mind after you've had a chance to reflect on what you accomplished?

Bachman: "The first game after I broke into the NHL [against Phoenix], it takes a little bit of time to really set in that you've even played in an NHL game let alone be successful in it. I think it really comes back for me on all the times that I go to the rink and work hard and try and get better and trusting that the process has made me a better goalie. So when I do get those opportunities, I'm not thinking about this or that. For me, hockey, whether at the junior level, college, and minor league or pros, it's all the same sport. We grow up learning the same sport, and you just have to trust that you've put in the time in practice, and when it does happen, you don't have to think about it, your body is going to react. You know what to do, and it's still the same game, just at a little bit of a faster pace. So all of that time I put in, it made me ready to have success. I think another good example was after last season when I got called up and won my first three main starts, and at the time, you're living in the moment and you're not thinking about anything. Then you really reflect, and you're like OK, some of that stuff I was doing out there came from a couple years back when I was practicing in the coast and trying to get better every day and trying to learn the position at a higher level. I think when you take everything and all the setbacks and successes at the other levels, it really helps propel you forward to be successful."

Goldman: I can remember scouting you during your years at Colorado College and there were a lot more highs than lows. But was there ever a time in your college or pro career where you experienced some desolate times emotionally, or you were just really frustrated with your game? If so, how did you manage that and bounce back?

Bachman: "There were plenty of times where I had that feeling. I remember when I was in Boise [ECHL], there was two weekends where we played three games in three nights. No matter what I was doing that weekend, for some reason, I just couldn't stop anything. It wasn't for a lack of trying or anything like that, I just couldn't stop anything. Those are the hardest times because then you go into practice and try to battle out of it. But for me, how I deal with the setbacks is by keeping everything even-keeled. A lot of that comes with preparation. I know if I do everything the same way and prepare the same way, a majority of the time, that will give me the best chance of being successful. So when I was going through that rough stretch and things weren't going great in Boise or Austin, I just continued to stick with what I knew and how I've always prepared for the last eight years. I knew if I just stuck with that and kept working hard, it was just a matter of time before I'd have success again. I think that's the attitude and mindset I've had, and it continues to drive me to be successful."

Goldman: When it comes to managing your confidence or dealing with pressure in tough situations, how do you handle this in the bigger games, like the one you had against Henrik Lundqvist in Madison Square Garden?

Bachman: "When I was first called up, there were a lot of different emotions and there wasn't a lot of time to think about it. Just like the previous question, where you work yourself out of a bad stretch, for me, it's all in the preparation. There will be times where you'll have butterflies and you'll be nervous. But I always tell myself that if you're not nervous, it means you probably don't care about it enough. This may not be true for everyone, but for the most part, if you think of all the times you're nervous, it's probably because you care about something. So I recognize that there's a healthy reason for the nerves, and then I just stick with what I know, focus on my mental preparation, and key in on the cues and the positive reinforcement. I get that going, and since I've been doing it for a while now, when I visualize things and say the mental cues in my head, it triggers something in my body, and it knows it's time to just go play hockey. Once the games get going, all the nerves leave, and you're right into the same routine you're used to. On the big stage, you just want to be consistent and give your team the chance to win. Do all of this, and I know that eventually the nerves disappear and you have a good chance to be successful."

Goldman: All I hear about these days is how bigger goalies are more valuable. But I know that there will always be a place for smaller goalies because they have to be smarter and quicker. So in many instances, they're usually more talented, both mentally and technically. Talk about how being a smaller goalie hasn't held you back in your journey to being an NHL goalie.

Bachman: "Dealing with a lack of size is something I've been carrying around for a while. Growing up, it wasn't a big deal. My family was never big and nobody played hockey before me, so nobody knew if I was going to be too small. In fact, I didn't really start hearing about it until I was in the juniors, then definitely in college I heard about it more, so it was definitely something I've battled with recently. Most of it has come in the past three years, ever since I turned pro. The moment I signed my first contract, the next sentence I heard was, 'he's only 5-10 so he may not be successful.' This is something I've had to work on, to kind of prove to people that it doesn't matter, and as I go along further and further, I hear it associated less and less with my name. It will always be there and it's something I'll battle all the time, but for me, I think I'm big enough to fill the net. For most of the goals I allow, rarely do they beat me above my shoulders, so I don't let it bother me. I know the net's not getting any bigger, so I don't have to worry about that. So it gives me extra motivation to prove people wrong. The way I've been able to do that is by being able to read plays and be a little bit quicker on my feet, so I can be a half-foot out further than the big guys who sit back a little more. Or I'll read a pass a little quicker so I can get there in time."

Goldman: What are one or two of the really important emotional or mental lessons that you've learned in life as a pro goalie?

Bachman: "I think the one thing I've learned about being a pro is the importance of making sure you show up every day to compete. I've learned to really get a grasp of how lucky I am to be playing a sport for a living, to be having fun every day. I have learned to take advantage of it, because it may not last very long, and so I've learned to enjoy it while it's here and have fun with it every day. Another thing I've learned is from my parents. They never put so much pressure on me to be good or to make it in hockey, they just wanted me to have fun and enjoy it. I think that was huge because if I had that external pressure to be so good all the time, I don't think I would have enjoyed it and wanted to continue to play for as long as I have. So I think that was a really important lesson. The final thing I'd say I've learned as a pro is that you have to enjoy life. You can't get so caught up in playing that you don't enjoy family time. Say I have a bad game, I'm not going to come home and take it out on my wife. I'll leave it at the rink and know I have work to do when I come back tomorrow. But for that time I step away from the rink, it's family and friend time, and enjoying a life outside of hockey as well. Especially in college, I got so caught up in doing so many different little things that it was almost taking over most of my life, where I was always constantly thinking about it, and trying to remember to do all these things. Now I've learned over the years that you don't have to do every little thing. I think it's important to have aspects of your game and things you do there, but away from the rink, it's important to have a life outside of hockey to enjoy."

Goldman: That's one of the things I hear from a lot of different NHL goalies; guys that are a little older, they stress the importance of family life. Can you discuss that a little more? Balance is one of the main themes of our book.

Bachman: "Yeah, for sure. I was talking to my wife the other day, and we were talking about different stuff, and how I am after games and stuff. One thing she said is that after I have a bad game, I'll call her on the phone and we'll talk about it briefly, for maybe three or four minutes. That gives me someone outside of the rink to use as an outlet to vent for a couple of minutes, and then I just get rid of it and I end that part of the conversation with her. Then we can go back and talk about other things and enjoy time together and do what we do without having anything held in. I think it's important to have that support to vent on and know I have someone to be there for me. That definitely helps me achieve the peace and balance in my mind."

Goldman: Every goalie prepares differently for games. How do you mentally prepare for an NHL game?

Bachman: "Preparing for games was something I started when I was a midget, so 15 or 16 years. That's when I started to realize how important mental preparation is for playing the position. Like you said, everyone does it differently, so I think it's important to have something to fall back onto. For me, I do a little bit of visualizing the night before a game. Then everything else I wait until prior to the game. I'll do a little more visualizing, then some tennis ball routines just to get my focus and my hand-eye coordination working together. Then on the ice, I have those mental cues that I use. In between whistles, I'll even sing a song in my head at random so that I'm not thinking about what the score is, or how much time is left. That's one thing that has really helped me become mentally strong, is having those little cues to help keep me even-keeled during the game."

Goldman: I'm curious about how music has influenced you. Everyone is a big music fan, it's a huge part of society today, and you can generate so much internal energy from it. Has music had an influence on your ability to get up for games, or a tool you use on a consistent basis?

Bachman: "Yeah, you're right, and yeah, it has. I think on my drive to the rink before every game, I'll listen to one of like six artists on my iPod, but I only listen to them before a game. It gets you excited and feeling good, and I think that's huge. And like I said earlier, I'll just sing a song between whistles -- I think everyone has certain lyrics that can get stuck in their head, and I think it's such a good way to stay focused while not being consumed with all the little details that go on around you. I think that helps you stay calm and lets your body do what it needs to do without your head getting in the way. So yeah, now that I think about it, I think music is a key part of my mental game. Even in summer skates or in practices, I'll catch myself just singing along to a random song, but it's better than worrying about what happens next, or how I did the night before. Music kind of helps you get all of that stuff out of your head and lets you do your job at a higher level."

Goldman: Worrying is such an easy thing for a goalie to do. There's so much that can go wrong, but in the right state of mind, a lot can go right. I know that goalies of all levels fight with that negative body language. So besides the things you've mentioned above, how do you get the worrying or anxiety out of your mind?

Bachman: "It all comes back to that routine. For me, the least amount of worrying I do, the better I play. One thing that helps me not worry came from a goalie coach named Joe Exter. One thing he said to me was that goals were going to be scored; it's hockey. They're going to score goals, it's going to happen, it's all about how you focus for the next shot. There could be games where you feel great, but you give up three goals that go off pants or skates. But once you realize goals like that will happen, it kind of takes the worry out of it, and lets you kind of do what you need to do, and let the chips kind of fall where they may. You work hard, you prepare, and your body will do what it needs to do. So the last thing you need to worry about is something out of your control. By realizing that goals will be scored and bad bounces may happen, it takes that worry away from my mind, and lets me focus on what I can control and what I can do to help the team win."

Goldman: Being in the zone is this really difficult concept to explain, but you know it when you're in it. I just wanted to get your thoughts on that. Can you verbalize it?

Bachman: "Being in the zone is a place you always want to be, but you can't always be there. For me, it's about getting rid of everything around me. There are times I can remember where every puck is hitting you, or there's a back-door play and you get it with your stick. I think that's when you realize you're getting in the zone. I've had games where everything goes my way, everything is working, and you're making good saves. When I think back on those games, you almost don't even remember them, and you almost have no idea what was happening. You try to remember how your team scored goals, but all of that stuff leaves your mind because you're only focused on the little black thing for 60 minutes. That's how I would explain it, nothing else matters and it's a pretty cool feeling that I don't think most people will get to enjoy, but it's pretty special when it happens."

Goldman: Is there anything else you feel makes you totally unique in your experience that helped you along the way, or helped you trust the process?

Bachman: "I think one key and one lesson for goalies to understand is that everything happens for a reason. Did I want to go to the ECHL right away? No. But because I was there, I realized there was a reason for it, and there was going to be a good outcome. Secondly, you have to work hard at it every day. If you just work hard and you show that work ethic, I think that's the key for me in how I was able to move up in levels of hockey. I just showed that I was working hard, trusted in my ability to work hard, and then when I get the opportunity, I took advantage of it, and good things eventually happen. I think it's really important to just trust the process, then take advantage of each chance you get."

Chapter 11
A GOALIE'S LUCK

"Luck is when preparation meets opportunity." -Seneca

Do you ever feel like your good days and bad days happen totally at random? Do you ever have a streak of good luck followed by a sudden streak of bad luck? Do you have a fantastic practice or pre-game skate, and then, by a series of unforeseen and unfortunate events, you somehow tank during competition?

Why does this happen? Well, that depends on the situation. Maybe you were just a step behind the play, or maybe your defensemen were caught sleeping, or maybe you really had no chance to make a save on that particular game-winning shot.

Maybe it really was just bad luck. Completely unavoidable and inescapable, we may feel that no matter what we may have done or would have been able to do, there was no way to avoid the perils of this fate. For reasons unknown, some powerful invisible force is simply out to get you. It's some sort of sinister payback for something you did wrong earlier in the day.

Grow up. Nobody is out to get you.

But this still begs the question of whether or not luck is out there waiting to startle and surprise us. Within the sheer chaos of a hockey game, is it possible to guide yourself to be in the right place at the right time in order to take advantage of your next unsuspecting lucky break? On the flip side, is it possible to avoid certain invisible pitfalls that randomly weaken your ability to perform at the top of your game?

More often than not, young athletes attribute successes and failures to plain old good or bad luck. They tend to believe that their performance on the ice is simply a result of being in the right place at the right time, or not.

Young goalies buy into this notion because they fail to examine the series of decisions and actions that lead to a lucky or unlucky break. It is easier (and in following with human nature) to attribute our perceptions of who we are, how we feel, and the opportunities that come our way to external sources rather than internal tendencies. We believe that we can only reach our highest potential when everything and everyone else is aligned with what we desire. Unfortunately, hinging our emotional, mental, and physical well-being on the actions of others can put a massive road block on our journey to becoming an elite goalie.

Therefore, we cannot gauge how we feel based on the actions of another. Rather, we must travel our own route according to our own individual road map, all the while allowing positive emotions and a strong mental approach to guide us.

When we focus our attention on growth, or on the process instead of the product, good luck and bad luck become irrelevant because all events are part of the larger picture of our lives. When we practice, train, compete, or do any other activity that leads us in a positive direction along the path of development, we pave the way for opportunities to present themselves to us regardless of their form.

As a result, when we stay true to ourselves and our individual desires, we clear a path for opportunities. We cannot be sure when those opportunities will occur, but with careful and intentional preparation we can be sure that we will be ready when they do.

Everything happens for a reason. Every time you lace up your skates, remember that each day is a stepping stone, a small but significant part of the whole. If a random string of bad luck acts as one of those stepping stones, then does bad luck really seem all that bad? It shouldn't, because it should become quite clear that it happened for a reason.

That reason may be shrouded in mystery for now, only for your future self to discover, but with a positive mindset, you'll soon earn some good luck, and that may lead to an opportunity that could have only come with the bad luck before it.

With that in mind, always strive to perform your best during every practice and every game. By doing so, you will learn the same lesson that every elite goalie has learned; that within your preparation, opportunity awaits.

Now luck has no real bearing on who you are, and now you are free to write your own story of success.

-Valley

Chapter 12

CONFIDENCE

Coaches, sports psychologists, and trainers urge their athletes to play with confidence.

"Believe in yourself." "Play to win." "Hold your head up high."

Whether in victory or defeat, athletes hear these phrases on a daily basis and are trained to display self-confidence, poise and integrity at all times. These traits are the benchmarks of the strength of character that is often expected of those competing at the top level of any sport.

The Empire State Building is built on a foundation that stretches 55 feet down into the earth, roughly the same depth as the height of a five-story building. It is this foundation that ensures the stability of the structure.

Similarly, how deep you build your foundation will determine the stability of your game, in both a physical and mental sense. It is not enough to simply *tell* yourself to have confidence, just as it was not enough to construct the Empire State building on a cement slab only a few feet thick.

Instead, it is something that you must be willing to develop over time. You must dig deep and persevere to build the foundation of both your game and your character. Regular training, both physical and mental, is necessary to cultivate a deeper understanding of yourself. Through practice, you will build the foundation upon which you can build an elite skill set and a professional career.

That is one side.

The other is a bit harder to circumscribe. There will be times when, try as you might, you are unable to pull off that game-winning performance. There will also be times when, despite hours of practice and an undying commitment, you fall short of the goals you have set. You may find it difficult, if not impossible, to "believe in yourself" and "hold your head high" in these moments.

So how do you keep your confidence when everything seems to be falling apart? The answer is simpler than you think.

Detach yourself from outcome.

When you step onto the ice for practice, when you log reps during a grueling workout, or when you read and study for a test, detach your emotions and your self-worth from the end result. If your energy is focused only in the present, and you concentrate only on that which you are doing *right now,* you will find your confidence does not elude you.

This does not mean to not strive to achieve a goal. Rather, it means to recognize your goal as more than just an end result. It means you should realize that a large part of your goal is the journey you will take to achieve it. If you can recognize that as you set out to accomplish your goal, you will change and grow along the way. Perhaps you will find that the goal you set out to achieve has changed, and a different one has taken its place.

The natural process of growth includes the development of self-confidence. When you focus on the process rather than the end results, your training will become more effective and you will step naturally – and with confidence – into the role you were meant to play.

-Valley

Chapter 13

TALKING WITH BRIAN ELLIOTT

Author's Note: From a rarely-used NCAA backup to a maligned starter in Ottawa to an All-Star goalie with the Blues, Brian Elliott has already seen the dizzying highs and the toxic lows of a collegiate and NHL career. A student of Valley's and a key part of the Blues' success, Elliott was more than willing to share his vast library of knowledge on the mental game. Like Mason, Elliott has played a variety of roles with more than one team in his NHL career, giving him a great outlook on the mental approach needed to be an elite goaltender on a consistent basis.

Valley: With each goalie we've interviewed, we kind of started by asking why you wanted to become a goalie. What was it at a young age that attracted you to the position? Obviously the equipment is fun, but there's something else there. Can you take us through your experience playing and your route through college?

Elliott: "Well my dad has a story and I have a story, but my brother kind of got into it before I did, and I always wanted to do everything that he did, and I tried to do it better than him every time [laughing]. I was a player and I liked scoring goals, but I had a hard time coming off the ice because I always wanted to be out there. My dad always says he asked me when I was young why I wanted to switch to being a goalie, and I told him I wanted to make a difference in every game, and be out there all the time. So he said he was okay with that, and we'd do what I wanted to do. I think even from a younger age I was always put in net in road hockey out on the street because I was the youngest kid out there. They just asked who wants to go in net, and nobody would, and they made me do it, otherwise I'd get beat up [laughing]. But it was fun you know, stopping all the shots from the older kids, they could never score on me. Some of the guys I used to play with on the street see me now try to take credit for it."

Valley: You became a goaltender at a young age, so you're in that mode where you play and have fun. At what point did pressure start to come into your game as a goalie? Did you ever feel it, or did it kind of transition in your junior years?

Elliott: "I hardly ever played rep hockey. I played house league as a player and I was happy doing that because I had a lot of friends from school that were on my team. I didn't really want to go out for the rep teams because I didn't have any friends there. Once I finally made the switch to goalie, I started playing up a year with older kids, so I wasn't with my friends anymore, and that's when I decided to go out for the Select teams. Then I made that transition, but they said I should probably go out for Rep level hockey. So I was able to participate in the AA tryouts to get ready for the single-A tryouts, and ended up making the AA team right away. So after all of that, I still wasn't able to play with my friends on the singe-A team. I think I was 13 or 14 before I made a rep team. The following year, I went out for the AAA team and made it, so everything kind of happened pretty fast for me, and while all of this was happening, I never really had a goalie lesson. When I was really young and first started out, I went to a couple of really basic goalie schools in the summertime, but I kind of just watched on TV and would go out and try to emulate the guys in practice or on the street. I was just trying to be like Curtis Joseph, Felix Potvin, or Eddy Belfour. That's when it kind of came around for me, and then when I start playing at the AAA level, you start thinking you can do something with this, like maybe play in college or go to the OHL."

Valley: We talked before about how you faced a ton of shots when you jumped to the junior level. How did that help you out, as opposed to being on a stronger team, facing less shots, and posting great stats?

Elliott: "To this day, I think it's a blessing in disguise that I got cut from my hometown team, because they were one of the best in the league. If I stayed with them, I probably wouldn't have gotten noticed. Even the guys I got cut for might regret it, because they're not really doing anything right now. They went to college and basically sat on the bench there, so it's kind of crazy how that all worked out."

Valley: From there you jumped into college hockey, as you got your scholarship to the University of Wisconsin. But for the first two years, you didn't get a lot of playing time. How did you manage that?

Elliott: "I was so happy to be at Wisconsin. If anything, I was just happy with a scholarship, and if that was where my career ended, that was fine. I didn't think of it that way, but looking back now, that's probably what the outside world was thinking. But my dad called me all the time and said he had talked to the Kitchener Rangers and they wanted me, so if I wanted to come to the OHL, I could still get all the playing time. But I never even blinked an eye, because that's not where I wanted to be. I knew that Wisconsin had a two-year system, where you sit on the bench for two years and then the next two years are yours to run with. I knew that I was good enough to do that even based on my sophomore season, even though I only got six to nine games. So I was just kind of steadfast with that, and I didn't worry about it too much. I just knew that when my junior season came around, it would be my turn to run with it, and it all worked out."

Valley: We all know that you dominated your junior and senior years at Wisconsin, so we'll delve into a different topic now and discuss managing pressure. We often say that experience is the best teacher, and you learn what works for you. If you think about your development as a goaltender from playing juniors to now being an NHL All-Star, talk about experience. What has it done? What have you learned and what were some of the lessons that have been huge for you throughout your career?

Elliott: "I think a lot of the lessons you learn, you don't even realize that you're learning them, so I don't know if I could put it into words. I think just the experience in itself is something that you have to go through in order to really understand how you deal with them internally, and without even thinking about it, you just kind of learn a way to deal with good and bad things. Even from growing up when I was little,

I used to cry if I had a bad game and I let a bunch of goals in. I just couldn't handle it. I think every kid goes through those stages where you want to be so good that it takes up all the energy you have, and you sometimes break into tears afterwards. If you're serious about it, and you have that drive about you, I think for the guys that go places, you have to really care about it. I think you have to go through a little bit of that phase where you take games really hard and you're being overly-hard on yourself. I still go through that at times, and I'm still learning to deal with the pressures, because when I came out of college, it was a pressure-filled atmosphere, but you had a standing ovation after every game just for trying. The fans were really on your side and they were backing you because they liked the school and they were Badgers. But when you get to the pro level, if you don't produce, it's your job, so if you don't, you're gone. So it's a different kind of feeling. There's times where to manage things, you have to learn to forget about it. If I go home and start thinking about a bad game or a loss, or even if I had a good game but a bad goal against, I won't sleep. I think all elite goalies have a short memory. There's times after the game where my d-men will come up to me and start discussing goals, but I won't even remember goals at all, so I'll have to watch the tape because I don't remember it happening. So I try to have a short memory; tomorrow is the next day, and you just come out and work harder. Good, bad, or ugly, I treat it the same way."

Valley: So basically you're trying to let go as quick as you can, move on to the next day?

Elliott: "Yeah, because the bad experiences I've had are when you can't let go. Every good run, you don't think about your success, you just go with it. I think right out of college, when I first got the call-up to Ottawa, I tied a rookie record for consecutive wins. They were like, 'how did you do that,' and my answer was that I wasn't really thinking about it. I'm not trying to do that, I'm just trying to save every puck. It's not a game as a whole, it's just that every shot is a different scenario, and hopefully after all of those scenarios, you come out with a win."

Valley: Well that's a good answer and it's similar to what Backstrom said in his interview. He said he never met a man that was able to change the past, so you just focus on living in the present and you don't over-analyze things, so that helps us reinforce the same message.

Elliott: "Thinking about what Niklas said, one lesson I did learn -- and I remember it and anyone who is having trouble, I pass it along because it meant a lot to me and still means a lot to me -- it's on the same lines of that. We had a team psychologist who was with Edmonton in the Mark Messier and Wayne Gretzky days. When I was struggling in the AHL, we went out to lunch because I was worrying about things, and I was feeling the pressure of not producing wins in my first year as a pro. He said, 'What can we do about it? Are you worrying about it?' and I said, 'Well yeah, I'm worrying. This is what I want to do, and I'm not doing it, and I don't know what to do about it.' And he said, 'Well, how about I come over to your place later tonight and we'll sit down and worry together, and we can worry for however long you want. I'll stay up all night and worry with you if you want.' You laugh after that, and that was it. That was his lesson; what is worrying really going to do for you? It's counterproductive. I can worry all night about things, but it's not going to get me anywhere. So you have to let it go, because worrying doesn't do anything for you."

Valley: We often talk about goaltending being a process. How has the process evolved for you? Why has age made you better?

Elliott: "I don't know, that's a good question. Obviously time and practicing your craft and learning what works for you and what doesn't work is a big part of it. I think it's so mental that you have to learn how to manage that pressure. I think that's what goaltending is -- managing pressure. There are a lot of guys that are better athletes that played for however long, but they couldn't get past that mental block of handling pressure. Obviously it takes a lot of luck to get to where you are, but you have an opportunity, and you have to manage those opportunities. The guys that can do this successfully early on in their career, they just get better at it over time. I just think the life lessons you learn as you get older probably help as well. Going through every situation, I think you just get a little more patient with the process, and a little more calm in the net. You look at every elite goalie right now, they're all calm but athletic, and they come up big in the big games."

Valley: If we look at your career as a whole, during your second year in Ottawa, expectations changed a little bit and you got thrown into the starting role when Pascal Leclaire gets hurt. Let's talk about some of the tougher times you've gone through, whether it was during that stretch

in Ottawa, or your short stint in Colorado, or wherever you felt it. What was it, and what did you do to mentally get through it?

Elliott: "My first season in Ottawa, I won 16 of my 32 games, so I felt pretty good. I came up from Binghamton because it was an emergency situation for them, so I came in and just tried to play my game. Obviously I wasn't thinking about it too much, I just went out there and played and we won a lot of games. I think it really helps when you're not thinking about what's at stake. Sometimes that's why rookies have such good seasons and then they have the sophomore slump, because they have lofty expectations and they put it on themselves when they don't need to. My next year, I played 55 games and had 29 wins and played pretty good overall. The third season was the troublesome one, one where we had expectations of being a really good team. But everybody was gripping their sticks tight and trying too hard, and I got in that rut as well. With the Canadian media, if you struggle just a little bit, people start questioning you. When you're young, it's hard to really let that go because they're asking you questions that you really don't want to hear. You're trying your best to put those thoughts out of your mind, but they're putting them right back into your mind. So I think I struggled with that -- with handling the media and handling that situation every day. I didn't even want to talk to the media after practices, because I knew they would ask questions that would put bad thoughts in my mind. I think as you get older, you learn how to manage that and you can answer them as politely and as politically correct as you can, and then move on with your day. We struggled all season long and I tried to do my best, then got traded to Colorado and they were struggling more than we were in Ottawa, so going into that situation didn't really help my game at all either. I put even more pressure on myself down there because it was another opportunity, and if you don't do something with that, you may never see the NHL again. I probably could have handled it better, but it just wasn't a good situation."

Valley: Let me ask you this then. Is there such a thing as trying too hard? What are your thoughts on that?

Elliott: "I know for sure that I can try too hard. You want to do the best that you can for yourself and your team and the organization and the coaches. But it's just like your golf swing. You swing too hard and you're not going to hit the ball. Goaltending is the exact same way. You have to let the game come to you, and that's what you learn through experience. You can't go in there wanting the puck all the time, because NHL shooters are too good, and they know if you're in that kind of mindset. They can just throw in a subtle fake and pass it across and you're screwed. It's hard to find that balance. Then there are other times when you're feeling it, and you know that you're feeling it. You don't put any thoughts in your mind, you just have that flow. It's so hard to keep that going, however. But I think game in and game out, that's why the greats are so great, because they can do that -- they can keep that flow for long periods of time. I tried to do that last season and I was pretty successful at performing consistently every night. It's just about finding that routine that puts you in the right frame of mind, so that you go out there and stop everything. You enjoy that moment, you don't run away from any of that pressure, and you're not playing scared."

Valley: Let's talk about your game. Take me through your mental approach on game day. I know when you're younger it's like your laser focused all day. But what approach have you found that works best for you leading up to a game?

Elliott: "Leading up to the game, I'm a little bit looser now in pre-game skates, whereas before, I would basically treat it like a game. I think that helps you a little bit because I need to feel like it's a real game in pre-game skates to put my mind at ease for the rest of the day. So once I hit that ice, I'm 'on' and not still trying to find my game. During the pre-game or morning skate, I warm up and do a lot of stuff that I do for an actual game, and I try to get into that mindset. I do that for basically every practice, so it doesn't really change that much for me. I tried to just be as prepared as I can, take as many shots as I need to, get that good feeling going, and make sure the last couple of shots are saves. I think last year was good for me too because I had my wife and dog to come home to. So I think when you come home to that, it puts your mind at ease a little bit because you have to take the dog out and give him a walk before your nap, and you really forget about all of the pressures when you have something like that. It just helped me to relax. That definitely made me a little more comfortable on a day-to-day basis. Then I'm just really focused in the game, and I think I found a pretty good mix of being focused and having fun. I used to do my own warm-up by myself and never talk to anybody, and I would be over-focused and I would psyche myself out a little bit. This past year I played soccer with the boys and had some laughs and kept loose, then put my gear on and then roll through the same routine since college. I've tried to smile a little bit by listening to music or listening to the fans and get that good feeling that you're going to go out there and going to win."

Valley: You mentioned something important, which is routine. Routine is experience, something you develop over time, and something that has been tested. You know if you go through it before each game, you know you're ready to go and you're on autopilot, so that's a really good point. So if you're out there playing and you're focused and something bad happens or you get scored on, how do you mentally reboot? What do you do to get past that goal as quick as you can?

Elliott: "I don't know how long I've been doing it, but the past year I put a focus on it. I've always done this same thing; turn around, take a drink of water, tap the pads and the post and have that mental talk that you have with yourself. This past year, I've put an onus on one thing -- treating a goal against and a goal for the same way. Whatever happens on their end or on our end, I am rebooting mentally to basically a 0-0 game. I did have a good year, so I didn't have too many goals to reboot from every game, so I do it with our goals for as well. I turn around, same squirts of the water bottle, and I think about it real quick, but I wouldn't have a conversation in my head. I don't get mad and my facial expression doesn't change at all. I think that has a lot to do with it because if your team sees your body language change at all, I think that sends a bad message, so I just have the same body language with a goal-for or a goal-against. When I look up for the faceoff, I don't even remember what happened. Everything is in front of me, nothing is behind me, and I just want to be prepared for that next shot. That gets me in the aggressive and patient mindset that you aren't afraid of the next shot."

Valley: We talked a little bit before about confidence. In your opinion, where does it come from and how do you get it and keep it?

Elliott: "For me, confidence comes from practice. If I feel good in practice, that's what is going to get me through the games. If you're waiting for confidence to come after you win games, it's too late. I think that's why you put so much emphasis on stopping every shot in practice. If you make those crazy saves in practice, you're going to make them in games. It's developed and I think you learn that over time, which is you have to get that confidence and you have to work to keep it, and my way of keeping it is just working hard in practice every day. You can't expect it to just change in games."

Valley: We talked about life management. When you're away from the rink, you try to relax more. I saw a big change when you got married, and you talked about that a little earlier. That's probably something I would imagine that you've learned through experience, that you can't think about the game the whole time and you need that balance. Would that be fair to say?

Elliott: "Yeah, absolutely. I think when you're a younger player and you don't have a roommate or anyone to come home to, the game is all you have. Hockey is your life and you do it seven days a week and it's hard not to bring it home with you because that's what you're thinking about non-stop. When you have a little bit of an escape, it helps tremendously. That has been my experience. I don't know if it's coincidence, but even when Amanda would come and visit me for a week or so in past seasons, I am pretty sure I went undefeated when she was with me. So I think it's about finding balance for sure, and with balance comes comfort – that's the good feeling you get when you come home, and you take that feeling with you on the way back to the rink. If you think about the bad things, those are going to follow you around like a shadow. Sooner or later, a shadow is going to put you in the dark. Once I figured it out that the support system and balance means a ton, it really made a difference in my game and my mental approach."

Valley: That's great, because the last question I had was to discuss that support network. Is that something you need, the backing of different people to stay balanced?

Elliott: "Yeah, most definitely. I think for a goalie it's especially important because you can have bad games and everybody notices. It's a hard thing to deal with so without that support system, it's tough. I think you look for that in many different ways. Obviously you and I have developed a good relationship, and that's what a good goalie coach can do. It's just a sounding board and you don't give me too much feedback or anything, just listen and be that person to kind of lean on. A few tips here and there definitely help, but when you have a goalie coach within the organization, he can really get what you're going through and can give you a kick in the ass every once in a while. He can make you feel good about anything. But like I said about my wife and family, balance is everything."

Chapter 14

BALANCE

"What is joy without sorrow? What is success without failure? What is a win without a loss? What is health without illness? You have to experience each if you are to appreciate the other. There is always going to be suffering. It's how you look at your suffering, how you deal with it, that will define you." –Mark Twain

Physicists, mechanical engineers and exercise scientists might define balance as an even distribution of weight allowing an object or person to remain upright and steady. They would be correct.

Investment bankers and accountants may define a balanced portfolio as one that has an even distribution of wealth for the purpose of minimizing risk and providing stability to the individual or company. They too would be correct. Economists would define balance as the result of supply matching demand. Right again.

For the deer-like Himalayan tahr, found in the most remote regions of the world's highest mountain range, balance is the ability to survive on sparse vegetation at rocky heights of up to 15,000 feet — an example of nature's balanced perfection.

But what is balance to the developing goaltender? If we go with the scientific definition, we might say balance is the ability to meet the physical demands of the position. It means staying steady on your skates, staying in position, anticipating the play, and maneuvering your body accordingly. It also means developing the muscle tone, flexibility, strength and speed to stop the puck at all costs. Goaltending, at its very core, is the ultimate test of physical stamina, focus and of course, balance.

If we apply the investment banker's perspective on balance, we might argue that the goaltender is the single element of stability on any team. With his unique ability to make split-second decisions on the ice, the goaltender has the power to either slow down or speed up a play. Cover the puck. Clear the puck. Make a spectacular save that defies the laws of science. All of these determine the pace of the game, the energy of the skaters, the mood of the crowd and what the sports writers say in the next morning's game recap.

A balanced goalie also allows his teammates to take risks. With his command of the game, he provides his skaters with the foundation they need to perform on the ice. A confident goalie will often instill confidence in the rest of the team, a relaxed goalie has the power to relax the rest of his teammates, and a goalie that manages the puck well can clean up an otherwise messy game in his own zone.

Like the economy, the game of hockey is ever-changing and subject to all sorts of influences, including politics, media, regulations, rules and restrictions. For any team to be successful, it first must establish an atmosphere of balance. The physical requirements of the game must be balanced with the ability to effectively analyze and break apart its cognitive components. This in turn must be weighed against the need for rest and rejuvenation. Each player's energy stores physical, emotional and mental components, which are microcosms of the larger team. When each player's energy supply meets the demands of the game, teams experience greater success.

Like a balanced economy, a balanced team thrives.

Balance is found in nature as well. In the above example, the Himalayan Tahr survives and thrives because it fills a unique ecological niche. It has adapted to its environment and developed the characteristics and abilities necessary for the conditions in which it must live.

When a goaltender recognizes that he must develop his own unique skill set, he fills his own version of an ecological niche. No other member of his team can do what he does. No other player can fill this singular, integral and essential role. For the goaltender, it is this journey of development and his attitude towards it that ultimately determines whether or not he – and in turn his team – will be successful. If he embraces the journey, he will reap the rewards.

The Himalayan Tahr did not develop its ability to survive in remote mountain regions in a year, or even a decade. Centuries upon centuries of evolution had to transpire in order for it to become the species it is today.

Similarly, the goaltender must be patient with the process and remain focused in order to develop his niche in an effective manner. He must trust that the process is unfolding before him, within him, and around him. He must remain balanced in mind, body and spirit. He must draw his energy from the strength of his character and his confidence in his abilities. He will achieve and maintain equilibrium through focused concentration, enduring commitment, constant mindfulness and steadfast faith that his story between the pipes is written one game, one save, one moment at a time.

Balance, in this case, is neither a state to be attained nor a goal to strive towards. Rather, it is a way of being and a state of mind. It is the manifestation of a world view that values growth over superficial success, process over product and spirit over ego. Being in balance means we ride each wave in the ocean of life with courage and commitment and an even-keeled approach.

The balanced goaltender shows up every day. He puts his best foot forward. He gives it all he's got at all times, with all people, and in every moment.

When a goaltender can say without hesitation that he is strong yet flexible, confident yet humble and knowledgeable yet still learning, he can then affirm: "I am Balance."

-Valley

Chapter 15
DEDICATION

The dedication needed to become an elite goaltender begins inside of you. It begins when you decide to make a commitment to yourself to move forward in a specific area about which you feel passionate. It begins with holding a vision in your mind of how you foresee your life unfolding, and then it leads to a formulation of a plan to take you there. It begins as a spark that, when given enough oxygen, grows into a flame, from a flame into a fire, and from this fire, into a blazing determination to see your daily pursuits through all the way to the achievement of your goals.

To remain dedicated to your goals requires high levels of persistence and patience.

When you first make the commitment to the attainment of a goal, you must consider the multitude of directions available to you in order to achieve it. Like a roadmap, there are several possible routes you can travel to reach the same destination.

You may set out upon one and discover that there are too many barriers in your way and you're spending too much energy trying to get past them. You may stop for a moment and reconsider your path, and if so, you must have the persistence to remain committed to reaching your destination.

You must have an open mind so that other options may present themselves to you. But above all, you must remain faithful to your vision and trust that you will get there, even if it is in the most unexpected of ways.

You may be a goalie who has excellent practices, stellar games, and the strength of character to back your team up in key situations. However, you may still find yourself splitting time with your counterpart who, although capable of stopping a puck, does not consistently display these key characteristics.

If this happens, it is easy to become discouraged.

Perhaps you allow your frustration to cloud the vision you had originally created years ago. But if you expect to remain dedicated, you must persist through this setback. You must change the direction of your course so that you remain on track to your destination. In this case, you may decide to be a role model for your partner, leading by example and showing you have what it takes to persist. This displays a strong commitment not only to your team, but also to your position. After all, there is no better way to learn than by becoming a teacher.

Furthermore, what does every successful teacher have and what does every role model possess?

Patience.

You must be patient as your journey unfolds. You must trust that by showing up every day and demonstrating that you have what it takes, you will be rewarded. Do not try to rush it and do not try to take steps that you are not prepared to take.

Build a solid foundation, one that will withstand setbacks and allow you to continue moving forward. Have patience as you lay each brick, knowing that every step is an important part of the journey. Rise to each occasion and do your best; another opportunity is on the horizon.

So trust in your vision, maintain a dedication to your craft, and have the persistence and the patience to turn your dreams into a reality.

-Valley

Chapter 16
TALKING WITH ERIK GRANQVIST

Author's Note: Erik Granqvist is not only known as one of the best goalie coaches in Sweden, but as one of the best goalie coaches in the world. Currently the goalie coach for Farjestad in the Swedish Hockey League, his inspiring story is one that truly embraces the mental and emotional side of the position. His path to enlightenment has taken him to all corners of the globe, and his wisdom on the coaching and teaching process brings amazing insights into the world of elite goaltending.

Goldman: What inspired you to start teaching goalies at a higher level?

Granqvist: "In the beginning, I thought there was a lot I could do on the human being and the mental side of goalie coaching. When I went to become a coach 12 years ago, I didn't really know so much about the technique, tactics or equipment at that time. So my original approach was always focused on supporting them mentally and as human beings. Then I learned the technical and tactical part along the way. When I talked to goalies, what inspired me to start coaching was how they appreciated someone that gave them the feeling of support, mentally and as persons."

Goldman: How did this inspired approach come about? What was the thought behind being a mental supporter first and then a technical guy second?

Granqvist: "It started with my own personal journey. I quit playing hockey when I was 27 or 28 years old because I just didn't feel happy anymore. I wasn't in

95

touch with my own feelings. When I was sad, I couldn't cry. When I was happy, I couldn't smile. I had problems saying 'no' and 'yes' to things and to people. I felt like I wasn't in a good emotional state of mind. I lacked a good connection with myself. I was just focused on performing; that was the only thing that mattered. Every year, I felt more and more like I was a bird in a cage, just stuck inside myself. After some time, I started doing different types of therapies and met a couple of sports psychologists that opened the door for me to do certain things, both for my own growth as a human being and also to learn the psychological view of an athlete. I think after two years of discovering and studying this self-knowledge and things like different breathing techniques, I felt really good. I was motivated to share this knowledge, but still felt like it wasn't the end. I wanted to go even deeper."

Goldman: So what was the next step once you realized you wanted to go even deeper?

Granqvist: "At that time, I started working as a kindergarten teacher because I came to realize I couldn't play naturally anymore. The playfulness inside of me was always connected to a goal. For as long as I could remember, all the playfulness that you see in young children was gone. Whenever I played anything, I had to win. I had to achieve something. So when I started working as a kindergarten teacher, it was my duty to play with them all day. I just played with them for the whole day and made sure they stayed safe. At the beginning, it was so tiring. I felt, oh man, they just have so much energy. But after two or three months, I could easily play with them from nine in the morning until four in the afternoon. I was just living in the present moment and just playing in the sheer blissful creativity of playing. I was there for them as an adult when rules were needed and boundaries needed to be set, but otherwise, I just played and was one with the playfulness and creativity that children naturally have. I did that for nine months and then one day I woke up and realized I had re-discovered the natural playfulness that every human being has from the moment they are born. So then I went to the school, hugged the children and thanked them for showing me the beauty of being in the moment without being tied to a goal. After that, I quit and went to India for three months."

Goldman: Wait…did you say India? Why did you go to India after this?

Granqvist: "To discover myself even further. I spent a lot of time in long periods of silence. In India I met a realized man called Madhukar, who did a 'Who Am I' inquiry retreat. You ask the question 'who am I' to discover the 'I', the very source of being. Who is aware of the thoughts and the sensations in the body and who is aware of the breathing? These things – thoughts, breathing, feelings and sensations – come and go. But who is aware of it? It was these types of inquiries that I would ponder in my mind for two hours every morning, then two more hours in the afternoon. I would take walks and enjoy nature in between. In the beginning, I was kind of panicked because my mental programming since I was young was that something had to happen. I was reaching for results right away. So once again, I was challenged with the obstacle of performing for the sake of accomplishing a task or reaching a goal. To eliminate this, Madhukar inspired me to be present in the moment. Just be as I am. It took some time, but then it was total bliss for me. I was so peaceful with myself, and I rediscovered a natural happiness and freedom inside of me, which is always being in the present moment, but we often overlook it. Madhukar and I are still great friends and we enjoy being together for a week every year in one of his retreats called Yoga of Silence."

Goldman: What did you learn from this personal retreat experience that led you back to coaching goalies?

Granqvist: "After my trip to India, I realized that at the core of who we are as human beings, we are already perfect. Nothing has to be changed. The core awareness is as it is – it's totally free. I've read about this in many places, but never realized it for myself until my trip to India. So after that, I knew I didn't need therapy or anything like that to change my personality. I just wanted to focus on how I would share these things. I had an overflow of energy and love, and I wanted to share it with others. So I went home from India and started to work with children that had special needs or learning disabilities. I worked with them for maybe six months. It felt really meaningful because most of them lacked support from their parents, and you could feel the pain that they felt due to their dysfunctional families, or from just not having enough support from home. So after working with kindergarteners and as a teacher for children with special needs, I felt the pull to bring this awareness to the hockey environment. What do I love most in life? It's hockey. It's been my passion ever since I saw Pelle Lindberg on TV in 1980 in Lake

Placid. At that moment I knew I wanted to be a goalie coach because I love the position so much."

Goldman: Is this when you finally started working with goalies at a high level?

Granqvist: "Well I hadn't played for about three years, so I tried to make a comeback first. I started out in the Allsvenskan [Sweden's second-highest league], but I realized very quickly that I had been away from the game for too long. So I was immediately drawn to the coaching side of the position, and automatically started supporting the other goalie on my team. From that day, I was a goalie coach. I realized I had more talent coaching others than stopping the pucks myself. That's a long story leading up to this point in our conversation, but this is the honest background of who I am as a current goalie coach for Farjestad. In the beginning, the players probably looked at me like I was like a UFO in the sky. They seemed fascinated by me, and while they really liked me, they thought I was one of the strangest guys they had ever met. They thought, 'Who is this guy and what is this peace and love and stuff?' It was exciting for them, but I know it was also a little bit strange. But then they started to mention to the head coach and other players how I was such a good mental supporter, and after working with me for a short time, how they felt comfortable and confident in the net. It was at that time I started to realize that I needed to really study the technical part of the game. I played the old school style in the 1990's, so I knew I was behind the times a little bit."

Goldman: How did that learning process work for you?

Granqvist: "Well, when I first started to really improve my technical understanding of the position, I knew the game was changing. Francois Allaire and his brother Benoit Allaire started to come over and hold his camps and address the blocking part of goaltending, like we saw for example with J-S Giguere and many other goalies in the NHL. It was the beginning of that era, when the blocking became more prevalent, so we started seeing it here in the NHL highlights and in games on a more consistent basis. Allaire would hold goalie camps here in Sweden, so I'd sit and watch and learn as much as I could regarding his teachings. That's when I really became a student of the game and position. I worked really hard at this, almost 14 or 15 hours a day. It became my total obsession, and I was so passionate about studying the position and learning from school and goalies, reading anything I could get my hands on regarding Henrik Lundqvist and other goalies and coaches in the NHL and other leagues. I knew I already had an advantage as an emotional supporter for the goalie, so because of my previous experiences, I wasn't afraid to support a goalie regardless of their mental state or situation. That gave me the confidence and freedom to work with goalies at a high level in my own unique way."

Goldman: I have to say, your story is amazing. I had no idea you started out as a kindergarten teacher and went on silent retreats and studied meditation before becoming a goalie coach.

Granqvist: "I haven't talked so much about it, to be honest. I just started a couple of months ago and thought to myself that I could be more transparent and share more. If we have 25 guys on a team, even though I only work with the goalies, I think maybe a few other players will have the same kind of reflections about not being truly happy that I had when I was playing at a younger age. These type of things can easily occur. I've now been part of winning three championships, and I think it's great to do things together and support the guys so we can win together. But winning championships doesn't even come close to helping players become one with themselves. So for me, I started to think, why not share this with the world? I can still enjoy coaching in a way that will support a goalie's growth and awareness and skills. But beyond helping a goalie stop more pucks, it is inspiring them to realize the beauty of just being. The combination of freedom, giving 100 percent in your role, and winning together as a team is priceless!"

Goldman: So how would you explain to the reader exactly what type of coach you are?

Granqvist: "I like to work with the whole puzzle – human being, mental, tactical, technical, physiological, and equipment. I break down my approach for you and the readers of your book, at the root and under the surface of it all, I love the goalie as a person. I really appreciate goalies as human beings, they are fantastic. But on the surface, for a couple of hours a day, we just work really hard on the technical and developmental aspect of the position. I ask them for their goals and what kind of coaching they want and how they want to be supported. For example, I ask them how they want me to be when they're lazy. I ask them what they need, what they want, and what expectations they have for me as a coach. Then I can support them in that way. After a performance, we analyze what was good, we look at what we can do differently, and what things we can work on. We work on the ice to develop what we see. After that, we may not have won every game or the league championship, but I always make sure to address to every goalie that they're still a wonderful person. When we do something on the ice, in the gym, or video analysis, we do it 100 percent. We take full responsibility in our role, which is stopping the pucks, being totally involved and helping the team. This kind of approach is natural for me, otherwise it wouldn't be worth it for me to be a coach. They do it for themselves and for the team, not for me as a coach."

Goldman: How exactly did you channel your past experiences in a manner that allowed goalies to process your teachings in a way that also improved their on-ice game?

Granqvist: "I had gained so much knowledge on the technical and tactical side of the position, but to take things further on the counselor side, I started working with a mental coach here in Farjestad named Lennart Carlsson. He gave me some great tools that I started to use on my goalies to help support their overall development. We worked together on different things, and came up with something that works extremely well. It was in the process of working with Jonas Gustavsson that we tried different things over time, but what worked best for Jonas was utilizing what I call open coaching questions like, 'How do you experience this situation in the net' or 'How did you see this play develop' or 'What can you do differently' or 'What other solutions do you see in this situation'. Whatever it was we were discussing, I always used open coaching questions so that we both assumed together that he already had the knowledge and the answers inside him. I just used different questions in different ways to make him search and find the answers inside of himself. Ninety-nine percent of the time, he said, 'Oh yeah, I see now...I could have done this.' From there, we'd imagine himself, see himself and feel himself using those alternative techniques or tactics, then move on to the next situation. Every game we'd watch every situation he was in, and if it was something we wanted him to keep doing, great. If it was something we thought he could do differently, we just asked those open coaching questions and looked at alternatives that forced him to think and find new answers. I'd ask him to visualize him making those new adjustments, or trying those new things. This kind of coaching method I developed together with Carlsson, and Jonas was our special test subject. The results were so positive that I kept doing it with the other goalies I've worked with. I've come to find that it's a very efficient method, due in large part because it is so respectful to the goalie. I don't say they have to do something, because if I do that, I take away their own natural knowledge and their own instincts for the game and the position."

Goldman: The theme I'm getting from listening to you talk is just the importance of finding yourself, and how that allowed you to support a goalie in finding their own selves and their own inner peace. That being said, how do you approach a situation where a goalie is clearly struggling with that, whether it's the way they move in the crease or the way they act off the ice? What if they are avoiding inner conflict and they are afraid to open up?

Granqvist: "The first thing I do is ask the goalie, 'How are you?' but I ask it with a deeper meaning and with full sincerity. Sometimes I ask this and they don't answer, which makes it fairly obvious they are avoiding something. If I get no response or a form of avoidance, then that allows me to say that I feel something is going on, and I tell them it's OK to share it. Then I start to ask those types of questions. I don't just leave them with that burden. It's not OK for them just to be shy and say everything is OK and then just walk away. Since I make that clear to them, they know I can feel if something is being avoided, so I say, 'I feel something is going on. If you want to talk about it tomorrow, that's fine.' Usually the next day they come back to me and open up about whatever is happening. Sometimes it has to do with the expectations they had for the head coach, or expectations they had for themselves, and they're beating themselves up about it. But once we cross that threshold, then I can start to support them when they open up. Another thing we use a lot with goalies before games is sheer breathing techniques. Awareness of the breathing and taking deep breaths to get the natural flow of the breath is extremely important. If something is kind of stuck in the goalie's mind for whatever reason, whether it is some disappointment or frustration, with better breathing, they can change the state of their mind. So breathing exercises is something I use a lot with my goalies. They take two or three deep breaths and then their mental state changes. Breath is the connection between body and mind."

Goldman: Do you have a specific example of this, or of a time where you worked with a goalie to make them a better student of the position and ultimately a better performer?

Granqvist: "I had amazing results with one goalie, but the lesson goes back to something I learned when I was teaching the kindergarten kids. With young children, when everything is not as they want it to be, they go on a strike. They stand in the corner, or they storm off the playground and they just stand in isolation and go on a sort of silent strike. When I would see this happen, I would acknowledge the child, go up to them, and without any judgment I would say, 'Ah, I see you're on a strike now. Well, tell me when you want to join again.' In my experience, it would take maybe 15 seconds before they wanted to join again. The only thing they wanted was to be seen. They wanted someone to see that they were treated unfairly, or someone to see that they were sad because something happened unfairly to them. So with older goalies, I started to do this same thing. With one goalie I had, if the first 10 shots were wrong in a practice, he went on a strike. He got really stubborn and frustrated and angry and closed off to the players. He was literally in a strike mode for one hour because the expectations for how practice started were not to his liking. The first time this happened, I said to him, 'It looks like you're on a strike now.' and he angrily replied, "What the fuck do you mean?!" Knowing I had touched a nerve, I told him the story about the children after practice, and he was still visibly angry when he went home for the day. At first I was worried and figured it didn't go too well. But later that evening, he wrote me an e-mail thanking me, that he knew what I had meant, and that he totally understood the lesson. The next day he came up to me laughing and hugged me and said, 'Thanks, that was amazing. I do this in my normal life too with my wife when she's mad at me for something. I go on strike and I shut her out!' I replied, 'Yeah, it's very normal for people to do this.' After that day, I just had to say the word 'strike' to him when I noticed it was happening, and he realized it right away. After just one week, I only had to remind him a few times the rest of the season. He had quickly become aware of his mental state, and when it did happen, he was able to take a couple of deep breaths and quickly focus on the next shot with clear focus. Soon enough, he was never on strike again, and from that evolved awareness, he was able to eliminate the mental obstacle of the strike, and became a better goalie as a result."

Goldman: Let's say you're working with a goalie playing at the top of his game. They do all of the right things leading up to a game, but all of a sudden the first shot they face is off a skate and in. As a result, frustration quickly sets in, and they're off their game the rest of the night. How do you help a goalie process and handle the fact they did all the right things, but within a game, things fell apart uncontrollably. How do you help goalies get over that?

Granqvist: "I've developed a teamwork with a great mental coach [Andy Sward] that was more like me in his personality, and I approached him with this same type of question. Goalies I work with right now use him as help as well. Whatever it is that is causing frustration, they can talk to him about anything, even about me. They're free to have a creative dialogue with no universal boundaries. Andy Sward has developed a range of mental tools successfully used within both sports and business based on each individual's basic personality. Aimed towards professional athletes we integrate our goalies into the BoostCamp.se program, which gives our goalies full access in using a range of mental tools such as the "Game Agenda", the "PreActions", and the "C-A-3". In the process of working with professional goalies we use these different methods to prepare, fortify, and program the goalie's performances. It is through working with him that we established something called C-A-3."

Goldman: How do you explain C-A-3?

Granqvist: "It stands for: Control, Analysis, Acceptance, and Action. Control means clinically, what happened? If possible, get good clinical feedback from your defensemen. Analysis means how did it happen and what would I have done differently? Always use the 'inside-out' technique. Acceptance means being honest and seeking the best reason to accept the result with the given circumstances. And Action means how to change or fortify your performance at the next comparable situation. C-A-3 can be done in a 'short' or a 'long' version. For example, on that type of situation you described, when the goal occurs, a goalie is trained to first take good control of the situation and clinically think 'what happened'. Well, it was off a skate and in, so it should be fairly easy for them to control their emotions since it was out of their control. Next, the goalie quickly analyzes it. What could he have done differently, what did he do right, and what can he analyze from the situation? Then the goalie must quickly accept the result within the given circumstances. If you cannot accept what has happened, then you will most certainly be stuck in the frustration of the result and damage your ability to focus and physically perform your best on the next shot or performance. Acceptance is the key, and when you do this over time, it becomes easier to look past it. Then comes action – the goalie should ask what they can do the next time something like this happens. The entire C-A-3 process might take like 15-20 seconds total. Take two or three deep breaths afterwards and focus on the next shot. We use it all the time, both in practices and in games. The long C-A-3 is most often done after a game in a calm and creative surrounding, like when we do video analysis. C-A-3 is also successfully used as a method to fortify good techniques or reactions and performance. The C-A-3 is the best tool I've found for a goalie to let go of the type of situation you described. Bad bounces or fluky goals or situations where you feel you should've made the save will sometimes happen. But when it does, remember C-A-3: Control, Analysis, Acceptance, and Action. Hence it will give the goalie the best possible condition to maximize his or her focus on the next performance."

Goldman: What is one "go to" tool you use to help a struggling goalie regain their confidence?

Granqvist: "If a goalie is really struggling, a fantastic tool that I use is to find video of a recent game where I know they liked the way they played. I'll pick out some clips from that game and have them watch the saves so that the goalie can see themselves when they're feeling really good. When they play the way they want to, and see how free-flowing they look and feel, showing them video like this usually works great. If they are really in a slump, I'll give them the DVD and make them watch the whole game at home. On the ice I create a common game situation drill where the goalie can build his confidence. I often record from different perspectives so the goalie can see how big he is and how much he covers in common positions. We also check that he is square to the puck and tracks the puck all the way. Mentally, I support them to give 100-percent and focus on stopping the next puck, whatever it takes."

Goldman: When you start to work with a new goalie or a younger one that is still a teenager, how do you get him to buy into these mental techniques that might be new to him?

Granqvist: "One super important thing is using the life story I told you earlier, but usually I wait to tell the goalie this until they are ready. If they are curious, or they hear from someone else about my trip to India, then I tell them. Otherwise, I don't impose my whole life story on them. I try to really adapt to the personality the goalie has. If he's someone like Salak, who was really seeking this kind of philosophy and new information and was immediately interested and ready to share these type of conversations, I'm all about it. But other goalies are not so receptive or willing to discuss these things, so I adapt to where they're at and try to open myself up and meet them where they are."

Goldman: If a goalie isn't interested in your life story yet, but you know he's coachable and receptive. Where might you start off getting him to be open to your coaching philosophies?

Granqvist: "In this situation, I start with the breathing techniques. With Salak for example, breathing was one of the biggest things he learned from me and it totally changed his perspective of a hockey game. Before that, he would get inside his own head and over-think things when he didn't see shots for a long time. But by focusing on the breathing, he realized you're now in the present and always in the moment. I always make sure to tell my goalies that many people could live their whole life without being aware of their breathing, but the best athletes I've coached and read about, they manage their breathing really well. So I try to sell this idea to the goalie. I tell them just to try it, and if they like it, keep it up. I never force them to do it. All of my goalies have loved it however, because it's so universally important."

Goldman: Aside from breathing techniques, how else do you enhance a goalie's awareness? Do you find that certain things work for a while, then fade away?

Granqvist: "Every month, we write down our goals and some of the things goalies want to accomplish. But some goalies don't like writing, so in that situation, we talk about the goals instead. That way they don't have to write, we can just sit down and talk and still accomplish the same thing. It's not that they have to do anything per se – it's more like I'm providing the goalie with a set of tools for their own life and to support their performance. If they don't like it after a few days or a week, we will find something else. The tools I used five years ago, while some are still in use, I've learned that many new ones have to come about because every goalie I work with is different. But this is a good thing because it allows us to learn from each other. This leads to new tools and new ideas every year. So it's not a set of fixed tools that the goalie must accomplish when they work with me, but rather I try to inspire them and tell a story to back whatever tool is on the table."

Goldman: Some kids are just completely un-coachable no matter how hard you try to get through to them. Was there ever a time where you realized that maybe you were using too many tools, or a time where none of the tools were working? If so, how did you handle that situation for yourself?

Granqvist: "It's a great question, but a complex one. I have tools that seem to work very well with many goalies I've coached. But at the same time, I strive to be like a blank sheet of paper so that I can really respond to their reality. I still run into situations where I feel like I'm using old concepts. A tool is a concept in a way, and I feel like if that tool is not alive, then it becomes dead. It's like having a bird in your hand. It's beautiful at first, but if you keep it inside your hands for too long, when you open it a few days later, it's dead. A tool has to be a living entity, and sometimes what happens is that I have to remind myself that certain things simply don't work with a goalie. The problem as a coach is that it's easy to start to project things onto a student. For example, in my own personal experience, it's easier for me to like certain goalies if they reflect a super serious and super dedicated personality."

Goldman: So what happens when you have a student that isn't always super serious, but is still very much an elite talent and has the capability of winning games?

Granqvist: "If I have a student that is a little casual, lacks a little determination and commitment, but he has other super good qualities like being calm, then it's really important for me to not project and think negatively if I see things I personally don't like. If I start to project a lot of my own shadow side onto him, then we'll have a problem because he's going to feel that I don't really like him. This is a deep answer, but it's important for me to understand the type of personality that I'm working with. Even if it's not a favorite of mine, or nor who I would choose as a good friend, I still have to be clear and not project shadows, because then our relationship will be negatively impacted. So I have to be alert about myself and focus on what I like about his personality."

Goldman: How do you get to know a goalie's personality, or rather, how do you get to know how he sees himself when he performs in practice or a game?

Granqvist: "I sometimes use a tool called an Evaluation Card after practice. I give the goalie a card and have him evaluate five areas that I feel are important, and then he grades himself on how he felt he performed in those areas on a scale from zero to one-hundred percent. Then, without talking to him, I do the same thing. Then we get together a few minutes later, compare the cards and discuss."

Goldman: That's interesting and I'm sure it leads to some great revelations. What is one of them that you experienced with one of your elite students?

Granqvist: "Well, for example, an Evaluation Card might start by asking, 'What is your dream or goal' and if the answer is to make the NHL, then we've established a standard. Below that question, one of the areas I want to grade him on is Compete Level. Say for example a goalie puts 80-percent on his card. Regardless of what I put down, I ask the goalie what compete level they think they need if they want to make the NHL in two years. And the goalie replies, 'well maybe 95-percent.' Then I reply, 'well, do you really think 95-percent is good enough to compete with the NHL goalies?' I start to talk like this and then most goalies say, 'hmm, maybe you're right... maybe it has to be 100-percent for me to even have a chance to compete with the NHL guys.' And then I say, 'yeah, I agree with you. I think so too. I think you have to be around 100-percent.' Sure enough, the next day we evaluate the same areas again, and now I find that his compete level is around 90-percent. It's much better than it was yesterday, and from there, the goalies usually start to rise to 100-percent, because they've enhanced their ability to realize this area of their own performance."

Goldman: That's fantastic guidance and amazing insights. What kind of feedback do you get from goalies when you use this technique?

Granqvist: "I think what I realize most is that they don't get this feeling that I don't like them, or all I'm going to do is verbally intimidate them or push them to go harder. It's more about guiding them by enhancing their own awareness. They said they want to be a top goalie and play in the NHL and win championships, so this practice today, what level do they have to be at with their vision, their focus, and their compete level? And usually they realize in their own way that they have to elevate their play. So once that happens, I ask them how I can support them to be at 100-percent in all of those areas. From there, you can start to talk about the different areas they need to improve upon in order to really compete at the next level. This is another long answer, but the challenge as a coach is when you start to mix up your personal preferences in what type of personality you like and dislike onto the goalie. He'll feel that right away, so if you can learn to be like a blank sheet of paper and not project things onto your goalie, then you will find your students will be more receptive. I've had these challenges with goalies in the past and it's pretty common. If you just push for results, it works for maybe 10-percent of the goalies out there."

Goldman: One of the other themes we've written about in this book is how a goalie's ego can get in the way of their ability to learn. I wrote a chapter about the importance of accepting when we're wrong. While we often feel like we're doing things correctly, sometimes we struggle to admit when we're wrong. How do you handle a goalie that is stubborn and has an ego issue and always thinks they are right?

Granqvist: "Fantastic question. I mentioned last time we talked that I developed a system with Gustavsson and started to ask him questions where the ego doesn't reflect so hard. So I asked these type of questions because I don't provoke the ego to defend itself immediately, and I ask them in a way that forces them to answer their own issues. Then they don't defend themselves, but instead they look for alternatives that could solve their problems. As long as they're willing to try and make changes, the learning process can begin. The kind of goalies you mentioned, they want to feel like they were the ones that came up with the solution and they were the ones that fixed the problem. They are still stubborn in that regard, but at least they have changed their behavior. When this doesn't work, then I'm the one that says, if you keep being stubborn with things that aren't working, whether it's a pre-game routine or a bad save selection that creates problems, then the head coach isn't going to play you. Then there is a consequence for being stubborn. This usually helps as well. I'll also use the best goalies in the world like Lundqvist and Rask to showcase how they do things to inspire the goalie I'm working with. Before I threaten them, I use the inspirational clips and stories first. But if they are still just stubbornly holding on to their own concepts, then it might be time to use a consequence of playing time to try and initiate a change. Usually they start to change and evolve to what is working better right now. Some goalies get to a certain level and their development stops. But if they would be more open and learn new things, they would adapt and would play at a higher level."

Goldman: So if your advice for goalies at all levels is to be open to learning, if a goalie feels like he or she is struggling in that area, what are a few things goalies could do to become more open or to be a better student of the position?

Granqvist: "Use the internet and watch the goalies that really inspire you. If you pick out a couple of goalies that really inspire you and see how they handle different situations, then you'll get inspiration from that and have the courage to try things like they do. Also, reach out to a goalie coach that you trust so you can establish and start a dialogue with him. Have conversations about technique and create a learning atmosphere together. But the first thing I would say is to watch the best goalies in the world and get inspired. They face the best shooters in the best league in the world, so watch them and watch how they handle different situations. This is a super good learning tool. But if you have a good goalie coach that you trust, involve him in your discussion. Then go into it and look at the pros and cons of these situations. So that's one piece of advice that I would recommend. The other thing touches on something we talked about earlier. Find something outside of ice hockey and give yourself some time every day or every other day to partake in those activities. Do things that make you realize you love life so that you value yourself as a human being, and so that your happiness doesn't only count on the result of a hockey game. That just creates tension and fear. When you do this, it's easier to give 100-percent when it comes time to compete in a hockey game. Stopping pucks becomes more joyful when you have something outside of hockey that also gives you happiness and relaxation."

Goldman: So far I've mostly targeted pitfalls, or how you handle goalies that lack mental clarity. Let's switch gears and talk about goalies that are elite with their mental game. What traits do you see, and what do you notice sticks out that separates them personality wise?

Granqvist: "The first thing that comes to mind is that no matter what happens in their private life, they have this quality where they can shut out whatever happens in their private life for those three hours, or during practices and games. Whenever I had elite goalies that had tough things happening in their private life, when it came time to play, they had this ability to brush away the outer circumstances and just focus on the task at hand, on the next shot. It became like a transformation once they put the mask on, and all of the distractions cleared away and they could be at peace with themselves and free themselves from whatever was happening in life. So that's the first thing that comes to mind. I've seen a lot of different personalities over the years, but the truly elite goalies also had some kind of way to relax outside of the game. Whatever interests they had, they talked about it a lot, and they knew it was a good way to escape from always thinking about hockey. They relax and enjoy life in other ways, whether it was playing guitar or reading a book or listening to music or going fishing. They had something outside of hockey that totally took them away from the game and put them in a relaxed space where they just enjoyed being. For example, Lundqvist talks about how guitar or tennis is important for him because he's not thinking about hockey, and the top guys I've worked with have all had something like that."

Goldman: One of the best mental quotes I've ever heard was from Mike Valley, and he told me that you play some of the best hockey in your life when you're happy. It's a great one-liner because it gets goalies to take a step back and realize that when you were a kid, there were no external pressures from parents or having to make a team or winning a tournament. As a kid, you always play happy, and I think that's

something Mike and I are trying to stress in this book. Those external influences really put pressure on a goalie's ego and causes them to be way too concerned with what other people are thinking, and that's seriously a theme I hope goalies come to understand is a vital component to being an elite goalie. So in closing, what would you say to goalies who are learning that lesson?

Granqvist: "It's wonderful and I love that quote, that happiness is your true nature. When you're in the moment, then happiness is already here. When you get too caught up with what will happen in a few hours from now, or what the coaches or scouts will say, you're caught up in the future and then you lose the preciousness of being in the moment, and happiness disappears. Be free and compete 100-percent."

Goldman: How do you explain to a goalie what it means to live and play in the moment?

Granqvist: "It's something indescribable, but the closest thing I can think of is that you are open and receptive to whatever happens. Your ears and your eyes and your five senses are in the moment, responding to what is happening. If you are off the moment, you don't listen, or you have trouble tracking the puck. Playing in the moment is thoughtless, and your whole system is ready for whatever comes. It's alertness. All the words can point to it, but it's something you can't describe. That's why I think sports is so fantastic because it brings so many people at the same time into the same moment. It's a spiritual experience in that sense because so many people are focusing on the same exact thing when it's a good game or a big moment in a good game. Goaltenders that are not present in the moment can run into struggles. If you're open to the moment and you're focused on the moment, you will play fantastic. Describing it like being a kid on the street is beautiful because they play for the sheer love and passion of the game, and for the happiness and joy of competing. Everyone has that natural state inside of them. Just give your 100-percent every moment to stop the next puck and help the team win. Enjoy!"

Chapter 17
THE TRUTH

"Man was made to sit quietly and find the truth within." - *Tao Te Ching, Verse 5*

Do we live according to our own truths, or according to those prescribed to us by others?

As dedicated goaltenders, sometimes it is difficult to sift through all of the noise and chaos in our daily lives and focus our thoughts on our intentions. With so many people offering advice and so many choices available to us, we can easily lose track of our goals. Instead of relying on our own instincts to guide our decisions, we put more weight on what others think we should do. In some cases, this proves to be beneficial, but in other situations it can be deadly. How do we know which path to take and whose advice to follow when it all seems so confusing?

In the Tao Te Ching, the ancient Chinese prophet Lao-Tzu gives clarity to this dilemma. He tells us to search for the truth within ourselves, using our own intuition to guide us and our own thoughts to direct our intentions.

When we are faced with a decision, we can listen to others and take their advice into consideration. But when it comes time to actually make the decision, we must search deep within ourselves to find the right answer. Sometimes this is easy to do and the right choice is clear in our own conscience. In other instances, we are confused, and our ultimate direction is unknown.

In those times when a decision is necessary but no clear answer is presenting itself, we must learn to withdrawal [see Chapter 9] and find a quiet place in order to focus our minds on what it is we truly desire. We must block out other people's desires for us and narrow in on what we desire for ourselves.

If we can learn to guide our thoughts in the direction of what feels best and good and positive to us, more often than not, the right decision will present itself to us without much effort. But in order to do this, we must make sure to focus our thoughts on the positive rather than the negative.

For example, instead of thinking, "I am not seeing enough playing time…" we must instead think, "I love being in the game." Instead of thinking, "I cannot make that save…" we must think, "Making that save feels really good." Instead of thinking, "my coach does not appreciate my effort," we must think "it feels good when my coach pats me on the back."

Do you see the difference? By putting a positive spin on our thoughts, we begin to create a positive flow that can only point us in the right direction.

As goaltenders, we are subjected to continuous evaluation by the media, coaches and managers, and sometimes by our own families. In order to maximize our success both at the rink and beyond, we must constantly focus our inner thoughts on the positive aspects of our game and our lives.

Our thoughts precede our actions, and our thoughts are one thing over which we all have complete control. Those who make an ongoing commitment to "…sit quietly and find the truth within…" will eventually find themselves in the perfect place at the perfect time.

This is not luck, this is law.

-Valley

Chapter 18
WHY BEING WRONG IS RIGHT

"Mistakes are, after all, the foundations of truth, and if a man does not know what a thing is, it is at least an increase in knowledge if he knows what it is not." —Carl Jung

As goalies and as human beings, we know first-hand that many days are emotional roller coasters.

While we may be considered intelligent, astute goaltenders by our coaches and teammates, we know there are times when we make mistakes or push the wrong buttons. In a game setting, we also know our mistakes are put under the microscope; they're often overblown and over-exaggerated. As a result, we know we must always be prepared to deal with the ups and downs of being right and wrong.

It's not always easy to admit it, but as goalies, we've all been wrong many times before. From technical things like reading plays incorrectly or making the wrong save selection, to training the body parts in the wrong way or wearing the wrong type of gear, we try to do the best we can, but we often make errors without even knowing it.

When Mike and I were writing this book, I spent a lot of time thinking about situations exactly like the ones above. Why do goalies misread the signs and patterns that take place in a game? Why do we behave differently when we make mistakes? More importantly, what does being wrong tell us about the mind of an elite goaltender, and how does it influence who they are and how they perform?

One thing we know for sure – goalies are proud individuals. We carry this pride with us wherever we go, but we all handle it in different ways. Some goalies like to wear it on their sleeves and exhibit emotional signs in an outwardly confident or borderline cocky manner. Others willingly choose to silence their pride by letting their play do all the talking.

Either way, because we are proud individuals taught to always stay positive, most of us do everything we can to avoid thinking about being wrong, or avoid the realization that we could be wrong.

And while seeing is most certainly believing, we must also learn that seeing can be deceiving; what our eyes process is not always reality. Furthermore, the fact that we may purposely avoid being wrong in order to "stay positive" is capable of being severely detrimental to a developing goaltender.

We all know we are fallible and imperfect at times, but when it comes down to making decisions during a game, we can't stand there and wonder if we might be wrong. Our initial instinctive reaction in the crease is a reflection of what we believe to be right, and what we feel gives us the best chance to make the save.

This is due to the fact we observe the game in a live setting. We make saves in the present tense, so we move and react in an isolated "bubble" where we read an event solely through our own eyes, and at that moment, understand our actions and reactions to be the truth.

This witnessing of game situations is easily translated to our mental approach. We are alone with our thoughts and our actions, and the way we perceive and process the game is not relatable to anyone else. Nobody understands exactly what we're going through when we react to pucks during a game – not our goalie coach, not our parents, not our friends, not our teammates.

As a result, we are left to process situations, observe our actions from within, and reflect on our per-formances all on our own. In the moment, we are fueled by our confidence to think that almost every read is the right one, almost every save selection is the correct one, and almost every reaction is precisely well-timed.

When we lack confidence and come to terms with the fact we are struggling or making mistakes, unfortunately, some of us are pre-programmed to believe that our mistakes are rarely our own fault.

It is not until after the game, or when we receive feedback from a coach or parent, that we can process the errors of our ways. But by then, it's already too late to do anything about it, so we find it very easy to sweep this feeling of being wrong under the rug. We are privy to executing our skill of "having a short memory" or "focusing on the present and the future" to let the unsettling feeling of being wrong quickly disappear.

Even when we practice, some of us are psychologically programmed to believe their own techniques are always the right way. So when another technique or method is presented to us by a coach, it often causes a rift when we don't agree.

Sometimes we think we're buying the right pads and masks, and even though they fit improperly, we lead ourselves to believe we've made the right choice, because we love the way it looks. Some of us use Extreme Step Steel because it provides us with an advantage with our attack angle, but some of us fail to realize or acknowledge the fact that it may also be degrading our skating ability.

We think we are doing all the right things when we prepare for a game (our routine), and if we win, we continue to do all of those same things, because we did it right at least once. But when we keep that same routine, and then we lose or struggle, we sometimes find it easier to blame the results on something else. Or maybe we didn't initially do all the right things, but we stubbornly fail to realize that we are doing something wrong, so we keep on making the same mistakes over and over again.

When we work off the ice, sometimes we think we do the right drills and exercises, because we are good at them, when really we are over-working certain muscle groups and ignoring other groups. We can squat a ton but we can't do lunges well at all. So we do more squats and fewer lunges.

The same patterns emerge and exist for nutrition, rest, schoolwork, and more. The list goes on and on.

So not only do we struggle with right and wrong in the moment of a game or a practice, but we struggle with the belief that our own methods are always correct. This hinders our ability to get a good, solid, well-rounded idea of what is right and wrong, including observations and advice given to us by others. And since everyone sees the position a little differently, this becomes a very important mental lesson for goaltenders.

When we make decisions in the crease, we make them with authority and confidence, because we feel like we're trained and experienced enough to be seeing the right things. Part of this comes from years of experience learning from elite coaches, or because we have seen other elite goalies do the same things.

We know what an active glove feels like because we've seen it many times before, and to see it once again is to legitimize the feeling of knowing we are right. We know what an active glove looks like, because our own bodies have experienced it when we play, so nobody else can tell us what it looks or feels like.

This method of self-talk and self-belief is a problem not only in our lives as goalies, but in our personal lives as well, because we grow up learning how important it is to "stay positive" all the time. Therefore, most goalies would agree that we often get stuck in this urge to force ourselves to experience the feeling of being right as often as possible.

This is what is known as Error Blindness; we have no internal alert system that tells us we're wrong about a certain move or save selection or reaction – not until it's already too late. We often find ourselves falling victim to error blindness, because as goalies, we know how bad it feels to be wrong.

It's embarrassing. It's threatening. It makes us feel vulnerable. It chips away at our pride. And no goalie wants that, because our pride is like our armor, and we need that armor to protect us from all of the potentially negative things we may feel, both emotionally and mentally, when playing goal.

Beyond the influence of our own pride, there's also a cultural belief that goalies should always strive for perfection. We know it's not attainable, but we are taught that we should continue to work toward being this perfect, refined, flawless athlete.

That's fine, in some regards. It's good to strive for perfection. But when we don't achieve it, we panic and feel we are doing something wrong, because according to today's lofty expectations of being a successful goalie, getting something wrong means there's something wrong with us.

That leads to an internal struggle, because to be right means we can feel smart and safe. It's easy. It allows the mind to be clear of any potential negative self-talk. It allows us to continue to play with pride and to play without second-guessing our style, our methods, or our pre-game approach.

But this is also why over-relying on the feeling of being right can be so dangerous for a goaltender.

Over-relying on the feeling of being right is an unreliable guide for what takes place in the world around us. It causes us to stop considering the idea that we could be wrong about certain things, and that does even more damage as we strive to develop our skills and reach the higher levels.

Further damage stems from behavioral patterns such as trying to ignore obvious mistakes, not being honest with what you see when getting good feedback, not listening to good technical advice during summer camps, and ignoring internal feedback from our bodies when we're training.

Again, this is a huge emotional, mental, and even a major social problem for us goaltenders.

Some of us may be more than willing to be honest with ourselves. Others may struggle. Regardless of where we rest on that scale, in order to get our minds to open up and be even more honest, we must think for a moment what it feels like to be right. It means our goaltending beliefs perfectly reflect reality in whatever situation we experience or imagine.

When that happens, we have a problem to solve. How do we explain this to someone who happens to disagree with us, like our goalie coach or someone who has more experience and knowledge than we do?

Do we assume or believe the person is ignorant and will eventually "see the light" and agree with our right way of thinking? Do we believe the person has the information to understand, but is just too dumb to realize we're right? Do we believe the person is actually quite intelligent, but we deliberately hide this for our own negative purpose?

Right in this very moment, be honest with yourself. Break the chains that bind your righteous mind and reflect on these experiences you may have had. This is important, because the only way we can learn to change our habitual thinking patterns is to acknowledge or come to terms with the fact that we may have been wrong.

This attachment to righteousness keeps us from being honest, not only with our own game, but how we manage and process our daily lives. In some instances, it may even cause us to treat our teammates, coaches, and friends poorly. We may become prone to turning others away, we may segment and isolate ourselves, and we may even create a dangerous rift in the chemistry of our team.

This may also destroy our ability to be open-minded and coachable students. And while we are not bad people for thinking we are almost always right, it is important to realize that we can no longer expect our minds and our eyes to be perfect "windows" that always see things the right way. Just because we describe events as we see them does not mean that's how we should expect everyone else to observe and process those same events.

In conclusion, what makes being wrong so right is this:

The most amazing part of our goaltending mind isn't that we can see the game and our abilities as they are, but that we can learn to see these things as they aren't. We must accept the times when we are wrong, because it is through the realization of being wrong that the learning process can truly take place.

To hammer home this lesson, reflect upon that last paragraph. Make it even more poignant by reflecting on a famous quote by Rene Descartes – one you've likely heard before.

"I think, therefore I am."

By merely thinking, you exist. It's a great quote that lays the foundation for many spiritual and psychological ideals. But a few hundred years before Descartes discussed the idea of his own existence, a man by the name of St. Augustine said:

"Fallor ergo sum."

That means, "I err, therefore I am."

Some of us learn this lesson of being honest with our own game quicker than others. But the elite goaltender is always open to the idea that they may be making wrong decisions, wrong choices, or bad reads. Even when they have mastered the technical side of the position, they are never afraid to admit their mistakes.

So the sooner we can achieve this type of mental approach, the sooner we will begin to improve our game and our ability to gain self-awareness as a student of the position.

We must come to understand that our capacity to make incorrect reads and other various mistakes is not an embarrassing defect or a sign that we're a bad goaltender. Instead, realize that it's fundamental to who we are, because we really don't always know what's right, and we don't always play the perfect game.

Instead of having an obsession with trying to be right all the time, we should focus on figuring out what we did wrong, and how we can do the wrong things the right way. This is the root of creativity and productivity, and it is how we can continue to be constantly-evolving formulas for future athletic greatness.

Furthermore, we can't be afraid to make mistakes. Instead, we must realize that it's only human to be scared of the feeling of being wrong. Once we come to terms with that, humility will set in and our sense of pride will fall by the wayside. This will make us better students, better learners, and better goalies.

At the end of the day, every game we lose, every goal we allow, and every mistake we make tells the same story over and over again.

"I thought this was going to happen, but this other thing happened instead."

This is life as an evolving goaltender; it is a fundamental aspect of the position and it will never cease to exist.

So for good or for bad, we must embrace the experiences where we thought we did something right, but the chaotic game of hockey suddenly alters reality and proves that what we did was totally wrong.

For I have learned that all elite goaltenders are capable of taking a big step away from that secure feeling of righteousness. In doing so, they have the situational awareness to look at the complexity of the position with the ability to say these simple words:

"You know what? I honestly don't know why I did that. Maybe I was wrong."

-Goldman

Chapter 19

TALKING WITH NIKLAS BACKSTROM

Author's Note: Niklas Backstrom was undrafted. Let that sink in for a moment. Born in Helsinki, Finland in 1978, he won a Silver medal in the 2006 Winter Olympics as a third-string goalie. Then he was the backup to Manny Fernandez during the 2006-07 NHL season. So it wasn't until Fernandez suffered a serious knee injury halfway through the season that Backstrom earned an opportunity to truly prove his elite skills on the biggest stage in hockey. He now holds the Wild franchise record for total wins (184 as of September 2013), the most wins in a season (37 in 2008-09) and shutouts in a season (eight in 2008-09). During the NHL lockout, Backstrom sat down for a quiet lunch with Goldman in order to provide an in-depth look at his own learned experience as an elite goaltender in the NHL.

Goldman: Start by talking a bit about growing up in Finland and how you realized you wanted to become an athlete.

Backstrom: "I think part of it was that my father was a goalie up through the junior-A level, and my grandfather played hockey as a goalie until he was 30 or 34, and he played in the Finnish Elite League. So it's something I grew up with since as far back as I can remember. We were going to watch hockey games and hanging out at the rinks and playing hockey outside, so I grew up with it, and that's thanks to my parents and my family. Like hockey and even playing soccer, everything was just being a part of what we were doing. That's something I was doing since I was two, three, four years old, so it's something you grow up with. I played soccer until I was like 14 years old, so I played hockey and soccer and all the sports was a big part of growing up. I grew up in Helsinki, but not in the downtown area, maybe 15 minutes from downtown, like in a suburb."

Goldman: So you spent a lot of time outside when you were a young kid?

Backstrom: "Yeah, I'm from that generation. I'm 34 years old now so we didn't have a lot of TV stations, just two or three different channels. We didn't have video games either, so we were outside every day. I have a younger brother – he's two years younger than me – and we had great games going on all the time. We were outside all the time doing different stuff, not necessarily sports, but sports were a big part for sure."

Goldman: Do you think your younger brother played a big role in you becoming a gifted athlete?

Backstrom: "Yeah, for sure. It wasn't tough to find a guy or friend to play with every day, but when you play against a family member, you definitely don't want to lose. You play for the pride too, so it's easy to become competitive when you have someone like a younger brother with you every day."

Goldman: Do you think it was important to your development that you didn't really play video games, or that you were outside a lot?

Backstrom: "Yeah for sure, but I don't think you can blame the kids nowadays. You look at the video games now and they're unreal, it's like you're almost playing something real. But for me, it was something where I would come home from school and go straight outside and play, and then go to practice. It was my routine, so for sure it was something that helped me along the way, and for sure I created a lot of great memories making new friends. I think doing that will surely bring some skills, but you can play whatever sport you want. They will all help improve your eye-hand coordination, so yeah it was a big help for me."

Goldman: So you must have become competitive fairly early. How did that transition to goaltending when you finally strapped on the pads?

Backstrom: "I think it's something that, well I don't know if it's my strength, but something where I realized how much I hate to lose. You don't want to lose a board game, you don't want to lose a card game, and you don't want to lose at any-thing. But being competitive for me is more than just hating to lose. It's more like what I'm ready to do to not lose again. I think it's something where, if I lost to my brother playing tennis, I would go out and practice tennis so I wouldn't lose again. It was something inside me, something that said I wasn't going to give up and accept defeat. I think that's part of it — you can hate to lose, but you have to be willing to do whatever it takes to win and get better. You can't be willing to give up and accept defeat."

Goldman: That inner drive to always want to win is an important mental trait for readers to understand. To me, it's a form of stubborn-ness, where if we lose, we're almost in a bad mood and it changes the way we live. Can you try to explain how you would feel when you would lose to your brother? I mean, what exactly was it, mentally and emotionally speaking, that inspired you to work harder?

Backstrom: "When you lose, you get pissed off. So it's just like an inner drive to be the best you can be. It feels like if someone is better than you, I don't know if it's a type of jealousy or if it's like you said, you're just so stubborn that you won't accept losing and don't want to lose. It's the same for me today. We could have a drill at the end of a practice and someone will score on me, but I'm stubborn and I stay out there so I can beat them and win the drill before it ends. If I lose a hockey game, I'd like to go out there right away and play it again. It's hard to describe that feeling. It's anger, and sure it's maybe a little disappointment, too. But maybe it's all of that combined, and that's what makes it what it is. You can get angry that you lose and act disappointed, but it's also how you handle it mentally that allows you to have that inner-drive to stop at nothing to turn failure into success in the next game."

Goldman: How would you say you personally handle losing? Do you handle it differently depending on the magnitude of the actual game?

Backstrom: "I don't think so. For myself, I go out there and prepare every game like it's the most important game of the year. It doesn't matter if it's the pre-season, a regular season game, or the playoffs; every game is the same for me. I've been doing it for a long time, so I prepare every game the same way every day I go out there. For me, part of it is preparing to be my best every day. It's a long season, but I want to play at the best when it counts, and that's in the playoffs. For me, the best way to perform my best in the playoffs is if I do this same thing during the whole year and prepare the same way during the whole year. It's a long run, but it's going to pay off in the playoffs if you prepare as well as you can in the regular season."

Goldman: So it sounds like what you're saying is that, to be able to be mentally prepared for a big game, you just keep the same routine and prepare the same way all the time. Then you just carry that same preparation over into the playoffs?

Backstrom: "Yeah, exactly. That's how I feel it works for me. It starts there and you find ways to improve how you prepare during the year by going off of what feels good. If something doesn't work, you change it. But for me, it's not like I want to change things from preseason to regular season to the playoffs. For me, it is just 82 games, and when you're in the playoffs, you don't think of it any differently because that's just game 83."

Goldman: So the playoffs is just game 83? That's brilliant.

Backstrom: "Yeah. It's the same game, but I mean, if I want to look back after 82 games, I want to make sure that every day, I've been doing everything as well as I can. If I've done that, I can go out there in the playoffs and play relaxed. I don't have to worry about something I should have done differently."

Goldman: So did it take you a while to come to understand that key mental lesson? I know you have a lot of international experience, but I also know a lot of these things are easier said than done, especially at an elite level. When do you feel like you put all the pieces together mentally?

Backstrom: "I don't know if I have all the pieces together yet. I think it's something you learn about every year. Sometimes you think you've figured everything out, then you learn and realize you haven't. I think that's a good thing. It's a fun thing to learn more about yourself, and to learn more about the game and the ways you can improve yourself. When I was younger, maybe around 20, coming from Helsinki, there were two big clubs and the biggest games you play are against your rival. So for sure you start to think about how these are bigger games. But at the end of the day, they're still two points. So when I was younger, for sure I realized these were big games and I had to do this or that to win, but then by doing that it usually screwed me up. I can't point to a year or a game exactly, I think it's something that just gradually happened during the early years. Every year you get into different situations and you get into bigger games. Or maybe you have a situation where your team has been losing a string of games in a row, and then you're in a big game for a different reason, because if you lose, something happens to the coach, or to some of the players or whatever. Or maybe you're two points out of a playoff game and if you win, you get in. So I think it's all these experiences that happen through the years and the act of going through them that really helps put the pieces together. It's something hard to imagine, or to think too far ahead about what will happen. It's just something that happens and you live with it. Sometimes your preparation works and sometimes it doesn't. When it doesn't, usually you stop and look at what works and what didn't and go from there."

Goldman: One thing that really intrigues me about the elite goaltender is how you guys manage pressure. Everyone faces pressure in their everyday lives, but for you guys, it's so different because you can't control a lot of the aspects of what happens. Can you reflect a little bit on how you handle pressure for the readers?

Backstrom: "It's still something you're trying to handle when you get older and you try to handle it a different way. When I was younger, that pressure came from outside, from other people. Now that I'm older, the pressure I feel is from the inside, from putting it on myself. That's been a big change for me and my mental game. When I was 18 or 19, I was playing for HIFK, and in that first year I was a backup to Tim Thomas. I played good in about 20 games, so the next year, they promoted me to be the starter, but I got hurt and I started to doubt myself. The exhibition games didn't go as well as they should, and Tim had some problems as well. But I think at that time it was a lot of the pressure from the outside that I let affect myself at that point, and suddenly hockey wasn't fun and I wasn't doing well. I think for sure that was a point in my career where pressure really affected me. It still sucks that it happened, but I'm glad it did happen at that age because I learned a lot. I think everyone handles pressure differently, and like I said, my pressure comes from inside now. But there's still a couple of things worth mentioning here. First of all, the biggest thing for me is the way I prepare. If I've done everything as well as I can do to mentally and physically prepare for a pressure-filled game, I don't need to feel any of that internal or external pressure, because I've been doing everything I need to do. Secondly, sometimes pressure is good to have, because it pushes you to go further, as opposed to being satisfied with something less."

Goldman: So you were able to differentiate between external and internal pressures as you got older. What kind of internal pressures were you putting on yourself?

Backstrom: "I think it came more from the desire to win. But to win, I have to push myself to be a better goalie and to improve my game and to do everything every day as well as I can. I think that's the expectation and pressure I put on myself. My goal is that, every day I go out there, I should be as prepared as I possibly can be. Never give up, fight for every puck, and enjoy it. I think all of those combined is the pressure of putting high expectations on myself. But not a day should go by where I'm not trying to improve myself. Every day I go out there on the ice, even if I feel tired or have all these different feelings, I put them aside and get the best out of me every day. That is something I expect from myself now, and that's the internal pressure I put on myself."

Goldman: When you have a lot of success every year, you're seen as one of the best goalies in the world. So how do you handle the expectations you have for yourself from the external forces, the fans and the coaches? Or do you try to block that out and consider it more of a distraction?

Backstrom: "I think it's a little bit of both. It got to a point where now I have a select group of people whose opinion I really value and trust, and I know that they are honest with me and want me to be at my best. So it's not that I go out there and listen to the whole world and care what they think of me or my game. It's more that I know there are a few people where I talk honestly about myself and the game and how I feel and play, and those opinions are the ones I really care about. I don't go out and read every newspaper article, I just care about having my select group of friends helping me, and I trust those people. One of the lessons I've learned in life is never getting too high or getting too low. If you go out there and listen to all the people talking about you, it's easy to get too high and too low. But if you have a few people who follow you for a long time and you really listen to them, it's easy to stay even-keeled all the time."

Goldman: One of the main lessons we want to discuss in this book with elite goalies is how you guys are able to live and play in the moment. Can you explain what you personally mean by playing in the moment?

Backstrom: "It's having a short memory and never getting too high or never getting too low. As a goalie, almost every day I tell myself that there's only so much I can do. I'm just one of the 12 guys out there. A lot of things could happen and go wrong and it's going to affect you. I think understanding how to play in the moment comes with experience and it comes with time. Sure you want to go out there and stop every puck, but sometimes it hits a guy's pants or skate and goes in. You can't do anything about that. You can't be a mind reader, and you can't see into the future. That's something I learned along the way. During a game, it's easy to move on from making a good save, but when allowing a bad goal, that's something I had to learn how to move on from. You can look at the replay up on the screen if you're not sure, and I'll often try to see if there's something I could have done differently. If I couldn't, I forget about it, and then after the game I'll go back and look at it again. It's not always easy though, because every mistake is up there, and everyone will see it. But it's a part of the game and part of the challenge, and as a goalie, it should push you, because you don't want to make those mistakes again. I don't know why, but it's funny that sometimes I think it's good to have a bad game or lose a game because that's usually when you stop and think about what you did wrong. When you have a good game, it's easy to move on. To live in the moment, I think that comes from just learning about yourself, and learning to know that there's only so much you can do. I never met a person that could change the past, and at the end of the day, that's hockey."

Goldman: So many goalies, especially younger guys, you can visually see how affected they are by giving up a bad goal. They tense up, they stop breathing, everything about their demeanor changes. They're so confident one second, but everything changes.

Backstrom: "I think for a goalie you have to look at it this way. If you let in a bad goal, are you actually any worse of a goalie after that? No – you're the same goalie, shit just happens. If you make a nice save, does that automatically make you a better goalie right away? No – it's just one save and part of one game. So bad goals and bad mistakes are just a part of hockey. Look at other NHL goalies – we all have different ways of reacting. Some of us drink water, some skate to the corners. For younger goalies, you just have to figure out your way to forgive yourself and forget it. Take a sip of water, forget about it, and make sure you are ready for the next shot. It's not that it just happened, but it's how you react to it and how you take the next step that matters. Are you going to let it bother you, or are you going to stand tall?"

Goldman: How do you handle the day-to-day emotions in terms of confidence? How do you gain it internally? Are there certain things that you do to motivate yourself and help you gain confidence?

Backstrom: "Confidence is something that goes up and down during the year. It doesn't matter what kind of year you're having so it's something you work with every day. For me, it's not about just a game. Sure, you gain confidence when you make some saves, but for me, I get confidence when I do everything as well as I can, and especially when I practice and prepare correctly. I can get it from a good game, but for me, confidence comes from knowing I've been doing everything I can to prepare the right way. Eating well, sleeping well, and practicing well. Then I have games where everything goes my way and then I gain even more confidence. But the basic confidence for me comes from knowing what I'm doing. I know if I have a bad week or practice, or have been a little lazy, I don't have confidence, even if I play well. So for me, it's more how I prepare and how I'm doing everything."

Goldman: Sometimes I feel like you can't always control confidence because if you can't control what happens on the ice, there will be bad bounces that take away from your confidence. So when your confidence is high and you've done all those things you talk about, when do you feel like you're in the zone?

Backstrom: "It's something you'd like to feel every night, but it's like you said, something where you almost know every puck is going to hit you. You can't see a shot from the blue line, but I know if I put my glove in the right spot, I'm stopping it. I don't have to think about it, it's something weird. Some nights it's just there. You just have the feeling that you're not telling yourself you're going to stop everything tonight, it's just a calm and comfortable feeling where you know they're not going to beat you tonight, no matter what. For sure it's something that probably comes by the way you prepare and practice, but on the mental side you have to be strong and really sharp so that your mind is ready for these types of games. You always feel like you're one step ahead all the time."

Goldman: Do you ever try and make it happen consciously, or do you just hope it happens and try to hang onto it as long as possible?

Backstrom: "Sure, you try it every day and every game [laughing]. It's weird to explain. It's just a feeling that comes from inside. It's not something you're telling yourself in your mind. I don't know how to explain it, but it's a great feeling though. I feel like if I go out there on the ice and I have to think, then I'm too late. Everything should just happen by itself and you're not thinking about anything, you just have a clear mind and you just react by yourself. Some days that happens, other days it doesn't. I don't know the reason for that, but when I'm in the zone, I don't think about making glove saves, it just happens."

Goldman: Do you feel like you do a good job of not thinking? Like you said, the moment you spend thinking about making saves, the time it takes to think is the time the puck is going right past you.

Backstrom: "I think I'm pretty good at it, but I think it's like I said, it's all about the process from the start of exhibition and training camp, even in the summer. I try to see as many pucks and play as many games because I feel the more games you play, the less you have to think. If you take a break or get hurt or sit on the bench for a week, at the beginning it's a little tough, but once you see a lot of shots, it's easier to not think. But when you see fewer shots and you have more time, you start to think more."

Goldman: One thing I've heard you say a number of times is that it's a challenge. So a lot of these mental obstacles you seem to treat it like a challenge. Is that a part of who you are mentally?

Backstrom: "Yeah, I'd say that's something I always try to do, to challenge myself every day. If this is the level I'm at today, I want to push it a little higher. Even in a game where you see a few pucks, it's not going to be like that every game, but it could happen in a Stanley Cup Finals game. So you better practice staying focused now, so you know what you're going to do when it comes."

Goldman: When you're away from the rink, what do you do to train your mind or enhance your mind-body awareness?

Backstrom: "I've been doing Yoga, not like every week, but for a couple of years now. I feel it's good for your body and good for your mind, too. But I learned when I was younger, it was more like every day you're taught about hockey, so at some point it can become too much. So I learned to know when I should think about hockey. I know I need to be mentally sharp and focused on game day, but if I feel like I'm doing that seven days a week, it's just too tough. So for sure there are some guidelines I try to follow so that I can leave hockey behind me. When I jump in the car and leave the rink, I leave hockey behind and get mentally charged when I show up for a game. It's easy when you have a good game to move on from it, but when I have a bad game, I try to watch the goals at the rink, then make sure I go through in my mind what I should have done differently, then move on from there. Sometimes after a bad game it's easier, but some nights I still think about it when I'm going to bed. I like to say, if you don't have dreams, you were never meant to earn them, so for sure, every player has dreams of wining something, so it's nice to dream about them too."

Goldman: So does that mean you do a lot of self-visualization?

Backstrom: "I do some, yeah. Hockey is a big part of my life, so for sure it's something I do."

Goldman: Talking to you here during lunch, it's easy to see that you're very calm, relaxed, and laid back. But on the ice, you have this very intense and fierce stare behind the mask. I see it with a few other goalies, like Nikolai Khabibulin. How do you put yourself into that mindset without over-doing it?

Backstrom: "Well, I think it's probably the way I feel like I need to be in order to be at my best and help the team win. I think every goalie prepares differently, and that's the way I prepare. I like to focus and be by myself, and that's part of my game.

I know if I try to be mentally at my peak on game days, then in between be more relaxed, I would burn out if I was always trying to be fierce or intense. So I feel for me, I need to do this to be where I need to be."

Goldman: Is there one thing you want readers to know about the process of becoming an elite goalie?

Backstrom: "I think it's going to take time for everyone to learn about themselves and what they need to do to be mentally tough. I think one thing is that you have to start by being honest with yourself. That's something that hurts for sure. It's easy for a goalie to blame a goal on the defense or just bad bounces, but I think you have to be honest and ask if you've done everything right in the crease. I think that's a big step, to be honest with yourself, and from there it becomes easier. Then you don't have to hide anything, and even though it will hurt, so what? It will only make you better."

*Author's Note: See our chapters on "Truth" and "Being Wrong" for more insights on this topic.

Goldman: Do you feel like you weren't always honest with yourself when you were younger?

Backstrom: "Probably not, so it was something I learned along the way. I think it's still something you have to work on. It's never easy to blame yourself for a loss. It's easy to say that, but it's another thing to mentally accept that maybe you were the reason your team lost. It's tough, but it's going to make you stronger too, so accept it, and do what you can to make sure it doesn't happen again."

Goldman: In closing, what's the greatest lesson you've ever learned about being a goalie?

Backstrom: "There are a lot of good lessons I've learned. From my family, I've learned about the work ethic, to work hard and never give up. But Mike has taught me before to never get too high and never get too low. I don't know if there's just one that sticks out, but you learn a lot of lessons as time goes on and you try to live by them and learn from them."

Chapter 20

THE IMPORTANCE OF DREAMS

"I have learned that, if one advances confidently in the direction of his dreams, and endeavors to live the life he has imagined, he will meet with a success unexpected in common hours." —Henry David Thoreau

You work extremely hard to earn rare opportunities to prove yourself on the big stage. Unfortunately, there's no way to know how that moment will transpire, or when that moment in time will come. For many, despite years of hard work, dedication, and perseverance, that chance may never come at all.

This could be due to a variety of things, including a lack of exposure in your location, unfair politics, or the inability to play well in a previous game. It could also be due to the fact that you just haven't been in the right place at the right time.

Regardless of the reasons, continue to trudge forward, but understand that fate is not always going to be on your side. Not matter how hard you work to avoid certain pitfalls, sometimes you simply won't escape them. Whether it is fair or not, some goalies get the breaks, others don't.

No matter what life tosses your way, one thing you do know for sure is that, when you do get a chance to play on the big stage, you must be ready. Every goalie wants to be seen at their best, but unless you are mentally and physically prepared, more often than not, you will walk away disappointed.

As you have learned, one way to mentally prepare for playing at your best is to spend some time visualizing yourself making big saves and winning big games in key moments. By doing this, you're reinforcing positive imagery and eliminating the negativity of fear and failure.

Beyond the role that self-visualization plays in your mental preparation, there's another way to establish the same type of positive foundation, but on a much deeper level.

Through the power of your dreams.

At some point in time, you have probably dreamed about successfully showcasing your talents on the most magnificent of all stages. Whether it's standing on your head against a superior opponent in the Stanley Cup Finals, or rising to the occasion after being thrust into the Championship game of your state's high school tournament, you know how those dreams have continued to influence your mood and motives.

To dabble in the delightful idea of your deepest goaltending dreams one day turning into reality is a big part of being human. It's not only a natural way to experience the passion you share with every other aspiring goaltender, but whether they are daytime dreams or dreams that occur when you are sound asleep, you always find yourself rising to the occasion. You succeed in a vast, movie-like way. You taste the sweet fruit of victory. You prove the naysayers wrong. You bring great joy and pride to your family and loved ones. You hoist the trophy, you make the desperation save at the buzzer, and you bask in that glory with your teammates. In those ephemeral moments, you get a little taste of what it's like to be exactly what you wish to become.

This idealistic and ethereal experience of being an elite goaltender was woven into the fabric of who you were as a young child with a vivid imagination. As you continued to grow into a more committed and mature athlete, those dreams have stuck with you. Even today, they likely continue to gain in importance and value, for they represent what you live and die for. They are a part of your true identity, and they are part of what makes you so unique.

Therefore, the main reason why you must embrace these dreams is very simple — they create a sense of familiarity for an experience you really want, but have yet to achieve.

This type of dream focuses subconscious energy on the very same opportunities you seek to have in real life. It acts as nutrition for your spirit, fuel for your mind, rest for your body, and it's something that nobody can ever take away from you.

You know you can't expect glorious opportunities to fall out of the sky, or for success to fall into your lap. Instead, you have to work for them. But you also know that you can't spend your whole life on the ice, so your ability to dream and visualize a successful future is important to maintaining and enhancing your dedication to those aspirations.

This is where things like meditation and journaling become a necessary part of the path to becoming an elite goaltender. You have to be willing to nurture your mind, body, and spirit. You have to be willing to strengthen your ambitions in ways that go beyond physical and technical training.

To dream of being an elite goaltender is to turn your mind into a magnet. The more you imagine and dream of yourself as an elite goaltender, the more likely it is to happen. You may have heard of this philosophy before – it's more commonly referred to as the Law of Attraction.

Simply put, by investing more time and energy into positively thinking about a specific goal or dream, you're more likely to eliminate distractions that pull you away from reaching that one thing you desire. By dreaming about it, you're getting a feel for it. You're reaching out for it. You're attempting to see what it's like to experience it. You're making it known to the universe and everyone in it that you want it really badly.

Beyond this basic law of attraction, when life does come to a point in time where you do have a chance to achieve that dream, you are more likely to be mentally and emotionally prepared to achieve success in that awe-inspiring moment. For, after spending so much time dreaming of this elusive opportunity, when it finally unfolds in front of you, you are guaranteed to experience what is called an 'aha!' moment.

This 'aha!' moment is a certain sense of self-realization, or in simpler terms, a type of déjà vu. It's a moment in time where you'll feel like you've experienced it before, but you know it was only in your mind. You *kind of* know what it feels like, what it *sort of* looks like, and maybe even what might happen next. It's a feeling of eerie familiarity, yet you clearly know it's a new experience. By knowing that you created this sense of familiarity simply through the power of your own dreams, you have some sort of fabricated imagery to help you play with a clear and relaxed mind in the moment.

And as we've explained in previous chapters, experience is the true currency of a goaltender's success. Without it, you have nothing. But as you gain more experience, you are better prepared to handle key situations in a more effective way.

Knowing that you helped create this opportunity through years of visualizing and working towards your dreams, ultimately, it becomes a powerful weapon to have in your back pocket.

Furthermore, this 'aha!' moment will not only help you embrace your destiny, it will help you appreciate the fact that it was earned. And once you've truly earned something so desirable, you establish a higher confidence for the future, because you know it was meant to be. You worked for it. You manifested it though a patient path of progress and development. By going through the maze of everyday life and by finding the right path needed to earn an opportunity to achieve your wildest dreams, you become fully aware in the moment. Your mind recognizes your surroundings, time will slow down, and you will not fail at becoming what you have worked so hard to become.

In closing, take a minute to think about all of the goalies you've seen win the Stanley Cup. At some point during the post-game interviews, they've all said the same sort of thing:

"I've been dreaming of this exact moment all of my life!"

So no matter where you are in life, always dream a dream and wish a wish that will never fade or finish.

Doing this will not only provide you with a stronger sense of purpose, but when the opportunity to perform on the big stage does present itself, your memory of those dreams act like a learned experience, making the moment seem less unfamiliar. And in that majestic moment, you will achieve success just like you always dreamed you would.

-Goldman

Chapter 21

TALKING WITH TOMAS VOKOUN

Author's Note: Tomas Vokoun is widely considered as of the most underrated NHL goalies over the past two decades. Whether it was with the Florida Panthers, Nashville Predators or Washington Capitals, Vokoun has consistently posted a solid save percentage year after year. What made Vokoun such a perfect interview for this book is his true identity as a mental warrior. Although it was not revealed until his playoff run with the Pittsburgh Penguins in 2013, Vokoun's ability to deal with a serious case of obsessive-compulsive disorder was a motivating and inspirational story that proved just how hard it is to be mentally tough and play at an elite level. At the time this book was published, Vokoun was dealing with a serious blood clot issue. This interview was conducted during the NHL lockout, but we continue to send well-wishes his way. We're very fortunate to have this personal interview to share with you and we hope you enjoy the read.

Goldman: How did you become an athlete and a competitive goalie when you were growing up?

Vokoun: "I think it all started with doing something I loved doing. Especially at a young age, I think it's very important to try sports, because if you really enjoy doing it, obviously you don't see it as hard work or something hard for you to do. You can't wait to wake up in the morning and go to practice, and if you don't like it, obviously it's not for you. When I was a kid, I played soccer and all the other popular sports. When I was six, I went with my friends to try ice hockey. Obviously I was playing street hockey and stuff like that before then, but I tried it on the ice for the first time and really enjoyed it. It's a funny thing to start, but it's almost the most important thing because if you don't like playing the game, I don't think you can ever really be good at it. I think for me, all the hard work is really something I enjoyed doing. I'm really lucky I get to play a game for a living, and I'm real appreciative of that."

Goldman: We all know that handling pressure is one of the biggest hurdles of being an elite goalie. How do you handle it?

Vokoun: "If there was no pressure, winning wouldn't matter and hockey wouldn't be fun. All of these things go hand-in-hand and you have to tell yourself that you want to play under pressure. People like to think that if you always deal with everything that comes your way, you're always going to be successful. I think that's a misunderstanding though. You can deal with pressure if you can adapt and learn every day. That's how you're able to overcome it. As I got older as a goaltender, I just found ways to put a positive spin on stuff. There's all kind of pressure out there. When you're young, you feel pressure because you want to play in the NHL. When you're older, you feel the pressure of providing for your family because it's your livelihood. So you're always going to feel different types of pressure and that's how it's supposed to be. If it matters to you, you're going to feel nervous and feel pressure, I don't care who you are. There's no escaping it. So for me, it's just being positive and knowing that everything in the world is not life and death situations. Hockey is a game and it is pressure, but it's also fun. If you learn and work hard, that's what separates you from other people. If it was easy, everyone would be professional athletes. You have to work hard and have a gift, and you have to be smart and learn and study the game, and learn from your mistakes. If you don't fix them, you're not going to be around for very long."

Goldman: Can you reflect a little bit on who you were in your mid-twenties compared to who you are as a mental warrior today?

Vokoun: "Well, when I look back at everything, one thing I know that you must have is life experience. If you're young, you just don't have it. You may be quicker or have better reactions, but you don't have the experience. You get that experience over the years when stuff happens to you, and then you try to deal with it and overcome stuff. It's a huge boost for your state of mind as a goalie to experience things. I always worked with a lot of sports psychologists and stuff like that, so I have routines and things I do, just as much as anyone else in the game. But while I have been trying and doing everything, and while it has been helpful, you just have to take what works for you. Sitting in a room and talking about something is never going to give you the confidence. You get the confidence from playing and succeeding, from overcoming things and sometimes failing and then coming back."

Goldman: I know before we started this interview you mentioned that you were willing to open up about a major mental obstacle you've faced throughout your career. Is now a good time to talk about that?

Vokoun: "Sure. I mean, I have OCD, so when I was young, I was battling that problem in the early stages of my career when I was in Nashville. They helped me control it and I talked to the doctors there and they helped me with it. When you're young, you're almost too much into hockey and you almost literally live and die by it. When I played bad, I was always down on myself and it was really hard to come out because I was depressed even away from the rink. But once you get a little older and you get kids and settle down, you do stuff differently. It's still so important obviously because it's your job – you want to do well because you're in front of a lot of people, so you want to be successful for those reasons. But on the other hand, it's only a game and you kind of have a bigger view of life once you're older. Even though I still love the game and I'm sitting here talking about it but not playing right now [due to the lockout], it's going to be really hard to walk away from it when I'm done. But on the other hand, it's just a game, and we are such a resilient species, so we can deal with a lot of different stuff. Some people choose not to, but if you're strong enough, then you can overcome a lot of things. It makes you not just a better player, but a better person. That is why you must learn from your experiences and see everything as a challenge."

Goldman: So with someone who has battled with OCD, how did you learn to keep things positive and not get depressed when things went wrong?

Vokoun: "When I was younger, I was making mistakes by not letting things go. That's one of the hardest things to learn as a goalie. It's different as a forward or a defenseman because you have support, and you can make a mistake and it may not cost a goal or you likely don't get singled out. As a goalie, you don't have that luxury. When you play bad, it's so obvious and everyone is looking at you and blaming you for the loss. So for me now, it's just about being able to let things go. That was the hardest thing to learn as a player and a goalie with OCD. Because if you're not able to do that, sooner or later you're going to drain yourself so much that you're not going to be able to play at your best. If you can't sleep because of a loss, you're dragging after a couple of bad games and you can't free yourself from that issue and start over, then you're not going to be able to be a successful goalie in the NHL."

Goldman: This is a tough follow-up question, but how do you let things go?

Vokoun: "Well I always admired goalies like Dominik Hasek – when he would give up a bad goal early in a game, he would find ways to stop the next 45 shots. That's a prime example of what you need to be doing. You just have to have a short memory. Sometimes you have to remember that and use it as a constant reminder by saying, 'Listen, I've done this before, there's no reason why I can't do it again.' I think letting things go is a lesson that takes time to learn. That's why when you're young, you don't even know how. Then you learn a little bit, and you start to think you know. Then you go a few more years and one day you're like, 'oh man…this is what it means!' It's just a process, you know? But you can't learn and can't get to be where you want to be until you go through the process. You know, it would be so easy to just read it in a book and then know everything when you're 21 or 22. But it doesn't work that way. You have to listen to your own experiences and be able to use it to your advantage."

Author's Note: See our chapter on the Four Stages of Development for a great example of what Vokoun just discussed.

Goldman: So once you joined Nashville and had this new approach, how did you become more consistent?

Vokoun: "For me, it was just a process. In my first two or three years, I battled inconsistency because I was young. I would have unbelievable periods, then very average ones. I think now that I look back, that's what I did to be really steady – I just kept playing and played for 10 years under different teams and in different systems. That's what I'm most proud of in my career. Of course I'd like to be talking about having three Stanley Cups, but I'm proud that I have been able to play at a high level for so long and in so many different situations, because for a goalie it's a very hard thing to do. Not everything goes perfectly or smoothly. Sometimes you run into problems and injuries or you play behind bad teams. But how you're able to respond and how you can come back says a lot about what you're doing and who you are."

Goldman: Talk more about the better balance you have now that you're a family man. Achieving balance is easily one of the all-encompassing themes of this book and being a mental warrior. Can you talk about that influence on your life as an elite goaltender?

Vokoun: "It helped me tremendously. If you look at my career and all the years I've played, the years I hit my stride was when I settled down with family and kids. They don't care if you have a good or a bad game, you just have to come home and be a dad and a husband. You can't bring that negativity home anymore. When it was just me and my girlfriend and we lived together, I would come home and I wouldn't speak for hours – I was just being mad and dealing with my OCD and thinking about stuff. But you can't fix the past. You can't change anything. Right after a bad game I would depress myself and make myself miserable, but it's not going to change *anything* to what happened, and it's definitely not going to help you in the future. And it's such an easy thing to say and everyone knows it, but it's so hard to do in real life when you know you're not playing well. It's the NHL, so you're competing with the best players in the world, and you know there are other goalies waiting for you to make a mistake so they can take your job, so it's not easy. But if you want to stay in the NHL as a goalie, you have to be able to forget about the past. It's just as important as knowing how to play the position and having the best style to suit your skills. If you can't forget about things and you can't start over and come back every morning with a positive and fresh outlook, you won't succeed."

Goldman: Most of us couldn't imagine playing under such scrutiny. How did you handle the stress, especially as someone who battles with OCD?

Vokoun: "I don't remember who told me this saying, but I always tell myself now that there are a billion people in China, and they don't give a rat's ass about hockey games. They don't care what happened in the NHL and they don't see the games, so it's not that important. So you keep that in mind and wake up the next day – it's a brand new day and you can't go back and fix anything. If you complain about it and push yourself further down the ladder, soon you'll get to the bottom and then you're done. For a goaltender, you play with a lot of guys and you see there's unbelievable talent, but so many guys don't succeed because it's hard to be mentally tough. I was fortunate enough to play for a long time now, so I know how hard it is. Some people are just not capable of doing it because it's just that hard. Mitch Korn told me from the start in Nashville that it's not a sprint, it's a long-distance run. When people tell you this stuff you might roll your eyes, but it's true, and it proves to be true over the years when you come to realize and find out who you are and how you can be mentally tougher. Sometimes it's hard to know what you're doing wrong, and you have to deal with it. People can help you, but it's still something you have to learn by yourself."

Goldman: You spoke earlier about how you've worked with sports psychologists to cope with your OCD. Between them and coaches like Mitch, and besides what we've already discussed, what's another one of the most important lessons about mental toughness that you've learned?

Vokoun: "Anybody who knows how I started knows this was my lesson. When I was 20, out of those 20 years, I had been playing hockey for 15. So I worked every day for 15 years to play in the NHL. I was playing in the AHL for the Canadiens at the time and I finally got called up to the big team. We played that night in Montreal and we lost the game. Then we were traveling to Philadelphia that same night for back-to-back games and the coach decided to put me back in. I had just been called up the day before the game, and you go, 'well this is my chance.' In that moment, I thought either I'm going to play well and stay in the NHL, or I won't and I'm never going to make it. So I get the start in Philly and I give up a goal just 36 seconds into the game. I got pulled after the first period after giving up four goals on like 14 shots and I was crushed. I got sent down after that game and I couldn't play well for like a month, even in the minors. I was just mentally so down on myself because I felt like my dream got crushed in a matter of 20 minutes. It feels embarrassing, too. People talking about it in the papers, and all of your friends and teammates and family are talking about it, so it was just so hard. It either breaks you, or you won't let it and you find a way to keep going. I never got called up to Montreal again, but I did get traded to Nashville, and I went there with a different attitude. I worked harder and got myself in better shape and I said, 'You know what, until they tell me I can't do it anymore, I'm going to try as many times as it takes to get back in the NHL.' For me, that was the hardest moment in my hockey career. But that short time span with Montreal pretty much changed my life. If we would've won that game against Philadelphia, honestly I don't think I'd be sitting here talking to you about how long my career has been. I would never want to go through that feeling I had after that game again, but it was probably the one thing that I experienced that helped me realize what I really wanted, and what I really needed to do to get there. Unless you're willing to do that after you fail, it's just not going to happen. So for me, that was a hard-learned lesson, but it pretty much saved my career."

Goldman: Just hearing you talk about it seems so intense. It also seems like every pro goalie I talk to says something similar, that adversity is a necessary component to success. What has this adversity taught you about being a mentally tough goaltender?

Vokoun: "Adversity is key, and once you get to this level, you must have dealt with it before. It's just a part of being mentally tough. For all of the great games and the embarrassing performances you have growing up, you're just trying to keep them as far apart as possible. For me, I think the toughest thing was to recognize that I couldn't control everything. You can prepare the best you can and you can feel the best ever, but you go into a game, an uncontrollable thing happens, and you will skate to the bench wondering what the hell just happened. Sometimes you just have to say, 'you know what, I can't control everything, bad things are going to happen.' I think the biggest thing for a goaltender is to be consistent. I don't think it's about playing unbelievable for three games and then being average for the next three because you want to know what you're getting from a goalie every day. If you look around the league, all the guys who are good at being consistent on a nightly basis have good careers because they're able to do it year after year. For that very reason, you have to be able to let things go, and know how to get through bad games. When you have them, you have to let it go and know you can come back. You have to believe that, and like I said, everything we've talked about is easy to say. But once you're out there and you know you've had a couple of bad games and the team is losing, and you know the other team is coming right after you, it's up to you. There's no help at that point, and yeah maybe once in a while you may luck out, but you have to make it happen for yourself. You have to breed your own success."

Chapter 22

WHAT DEFINES A MASTER?

"It is through the twin gateways of persistence and patience that masters become masters." —Mike Dooley, Notes from the Universe

What defines a master?

Does being a master mean that we are the best of the best? That we have reached the pinnacle of our achievements and are ready to sit back with our arms folded like the Buddha, taking a deep breath, observing all we have accomplished? Does becoming a master mean that we are now ready to pass our knowledge to others who are writing their own stories of success?

One of the definitions offered by Webster's Dictionary is "a player of consummate skill" and the definition of Consummate is "complete in every detail."

If we buy into Webster's definitions, it would be impossible to achieve a "master" status in anything. If we were to be "complete in every detail" of our lives, we would have ceased trying to improve ourselves. We could sit back like Buddha, observing all and nodding our heads in approval, but as athletes, this is not our inclination.

As goaltenders, we continually seek improvement over what has come before. With every practice and every game, we strive to play with more accuracy, stamina, strength and commitment. We "master" a skill only to practice it over and over again, perfecting our technique, making good even better.

The competitiveness and fast-paced nature of hockey requires that we are constantly on top of our game. Opportunities can come and go in the blink of an eye. We must always be mindful of the details necessary to capitalize on these opportunities and propel us to the next level. Even in the top leagues of the sport, there is a continuous quest for perfection. We all seek to become masters.

As you move forward, think about what you can do during practices, games, and all moments in between to maximize your potential. Pay attention to those details; not just on the ice, but in the dressing room, at the training table, as you rest, as you relax with your friends, and as you prepare yourself for the next competition.

Remember that it is the details that make up the whole. All of the parts must be present and functional for your machine-like body to perform efficiently.

So do not focus too much energy on being a "master." Instead, place your thoughts and actions on the moment-by-moment "details" that, when put together, form a complete and amazing whole.

———

There is No Such Thing as Failure, Only Results

There is no such thing as failure. There are only results.

At the outset, this appears to be a false statement. For example, let's say a runner sets out to complete a 25-mile marathon. He makes it only 13 miles before falling to the ground, totally exhausted. He lies there on his back, stares up at the sky and declares himself a failure for not having achieved his goal.

His desire was to run a marathon but he did not get to experience his desire. But what he has experienced is a result; he is halfway to his goal.

The runner catches his breath and rolls over in the grass. A small voice, one that only he can hear, tells him to keep training, keep running, and to keep holding the vision in his mind of what it will feel like when he finally accomplishes his goal. He gets to his feet and begins walking. He gazes at the horizon. He takes a deep breath. He sets his sights on his next run.

"Most people fail in life, not because they aim too high and miss, but because they aim too low and hit."—Les Brown

If our runner would have given up his desire to one day complete a marathon because, at present, he is only able to run 13 miles, he would not experience the sense of fulfillment that goes along with achieving his goal. However, if he adjusts his thinking and does not even introduce the idea of failure into his belief system, the possibility of never achieving his goal will not exist. Instead, he will view the 13 miles completed as a stepping stone, a result of his efforts thus far, and motivation to keep on going.

Therefore, part of what defines a master is having the ability to change our thoughts regarding any particular goal we wish to achieve. Rather than labeling ourselves as failures because we may stumble along the way, we simply have to step back and re-evaluate our assessment of the situation.

Instead, we have to see our blunders only as results. At times they may be undesirable, but they are always, without exception, results. If we wish to change our results, we must first change the behavior that produced them. But before we change our behavior, we must change our thoughts.

When we begin to change our thoughts and behaviors from those of either failure or success to those that simply generate results, we remove our self-prescribed labels of "good" or "bad" and begin to see our actions and their effects for what they really are; steps in a process that will inevitably produce a result.

It can be helpful to think of the process of achieving our goals (and eventually becoming elite) as a pyramid. At the very top, the pinnacle, is the dream we wish to achieve. That dream could not exist without the wide base of experience underneath it. Without a solid foundation of layer upon layer of carefully placed blocks, the pinnacle would collapse.

The steps to achieving a goal are like this pyramid. Each block in the pyramid does not consider itself a failure because it is not the crowning glory of the structure. It sits with all the others as a support for the entire structure and its position is very important. Without it and those around it, the entire thing would crumble to the ground.

If we can learn to think of our experiences on the way to achieving a goal as these supporting blocks, we realize that without them our goal would not be possible. Our experiences, or blocks, are not successful or unsuccessful, they are just part of the process we go through as we construct our own pyramids.

Before you step onto the ice or head out to the gym, remember that there's no such thing as failure, there are only results. Each time you do something that produces a result, you have placed another block onto the pyramid that is your life.

If you want to get to that pinnacle, the only way to do it is to keep building and strengthening the foundation.

-Valley

Chapter 23

TALKING WITH PEKKA RINNE

Author's Note: There's simply no denying the elite skills of Nashville Predators goaltender Pekka Rinne. With many years of experience playing behind a team that doesn't score a lot of goals, Rinne's mental skills are forged in fire and an amazing learning tool for goalies everywhere. We spoke with him prior to training camp for the 2013-14 NHL season and got some great insight on his mental game.

Goldman: Can you give us a real brief background on how you got involved in goaltending in Finland? How did you develop the passion for becoming a goaltender?

Rinne: "I think it all started with my cousin, who is seven years older than me. He was a goalie in my hometown and he was playing on the junior team, and I always looked up to him. So I kind of always thought it was cool to watch him play. We would always play street hockey, so when I was big enough, maybe five or six years old, they started putting me in the net, and that's ultimately how it started. It all started just playing street hockey and I grew pretty passionate being a goalie. I always wanted to be a goalie when we would just play on the streets every single day, so then I joined a team when I was seven years old. At first I was just a regular player, but soon after, the team didn't have a goalie, so it was a pretty classic story. They asked me if I wanted to be the goalie and obviously I wanted to do it, so since then, I've always been a goalie. At the same time, I do enjoy playing out as a player in street hockey or just for fun, goofing around. But I started at a pretty early age, and my cousin was my first idol, so I always looked up to him. He was the one that would pass his old gear down to me, and that's how I got started."

Goldman: What really started to motivate you to become more competitive as a goalie?

Rinne: "I think for myself it took a while. I was always passionate about playing the game and being a goalie. I would always watch a lot of other goalies on the Finnish national team and in the pro level of hockey in Finland. Once a week we would also get a little NHL news on a Finnish TV show and that's how I got to know a lot of NHL goalies. So it slowly became more and more competitive for me I guess, but it still took me a while to start working on my game. I didn't do that for a while because I played for fun for a long, long time. I always played on really good teams in really small cities, so it wasn't anything like a major level of hockey, it was just fun. But for myself, it got more serious when I was maybe 15 and I realized I wanted to take it seriously when I didn't make the first National Team. I didn't make any of those teams, so I think around that time when I was 15 or 16, I kind of realized that if I ever wanted to do anything with this game as a hockey player, I needed to work on things. So around that time, I started to really focus on hockey and take the training a little more seriously, and around then I got my first goalie coach. So it was 15, 16, and age 17 when I really turned it around. I had some good coaches for the most part of my junior hockey career, and even my first few years in pro in Finland. I had the same goalie coach, and that helped me to create a lot of consistency. I still talk to him today and work with him during the offseason."

Goldman: So when did you start to really focus on improving your skills and your mental game?

Rinne: "I think it took me a while to really start working on my game, but I was always passionate about hockey. There were a lot of other things going on as well, as I played a lot of other sports and took them seriously too, so I always dreamed big. Growing up, I always dreamed of playing professional hockey, but I never really thought that it would happen. Maybe if I made the Finnish league that would have been my dream and goal, but as I grew older, I set my goals higher, and once you reach some level, you set new goals, and that's kind of how my junior career went. I never really thought I would build up any huge expectations for myself, but I always knew that if I worked hard enough, I'd have a chance. Eventually, when I got a little bit older, a lot of good things started happening."

Goldman: Can you talk about how dreaming big helped you to stay focused on elevating your goals?

Rinne: "Well, I think it's huge. I thought that where I was from, there was no way I could end up being in the NHL. But you think you're so far away from the NHL and it wasn't realistic. But those things were always being dreamed about. I think it's huge when you set goals for yourself and you have to challenge yourself always. When I was around 16, I switched to a more competitive team, and it was one of my goals to be able to play for that team. Once I joined that team, I realized how weak I was, and all of those things became an eye-opening experience for myself on how much I needed to work on the ice and off the ice, too. I was really just a tall, lanky kid, and I never had even lifted weights or done any of that stuff. Even though I was always athletic because I played a bunch of different sports, it was a big eye-opening experience to see just how much work needed to be done. I guess during those years, dreaming big was a big step. I became a better athlete and I started living a more athletic lifestyle, basically playing more competitive hockey. The practices were tough and the summertime included tough training. So I think during those years, dreaming big and setting goals was huge. Even at that time, especially when I noticed my weaknesses, I really thought that, oh man, this is going to be hard for me to get anywhere and I have a lot of work to get done. But without the goals and without the big dreams, I don't think it would have been possible."

Goldman: You talked about how it was a real eye-opening experience during the years when you changed teams and started to realize you had a lot to work on. How important do you think that experience is for young goalies, to realize they have a lot to work on and they're not as good as they thought?

Rinne: "I think it's a little bit of a humbling experience, and if you take it the right way, it makes you work harder and makes you really appreciate the chance you have at that moment. You start learning from the other goalies and start looking up to the guys that are ahead of you. You learn what they do right to be successful, so I think for everybody, it doesn't matter how good you are, regardless of the junior or pro level, everyone is going to face adversity and everyone is going to have moments where they realize there's a lot of work to be done. Nobody is perfect, so I think overall it's a good experience when you face those moments. I feel like even though I'm in the NHL, I still battle with those thoughts, and at the same time they keep you grounded, they keep you humble, and they keep you honest and hard-working."

Goldman: On that same note, in terms of it being a humbling experience, can you point to maybe one thing mentally or emotionally recently where you've had that experience?

Rinne: "At the NHL level, I think my first couple of years I just tried to establish myself and get more ice time. There's not too much pressure because you just learn as you go. But yeah, the last few years, especially this year, as a team and myself included, we had some success in the past, so my expectations grew and I feel like I put a lot of pressure on myself on the inside to perform. This year, at the end of the season, you expect so much more from yourself, even though as a team we went through some tough times with a lot of injuries. We had a really rough last part of the season, and so I think it's at those times when you think in your head you can always help the team, and in the tough moments, put them on your shoulders. But when it's not happening, you start second-guessing yourself, so it's a good reminder that you have to do the best you can and you can't try to be a superhuman being. You can't change the way you are or the way you play and all of those kind of things. So I think even today, I'm always learning things about myself and you learn ways to handle different situations. I believe after the season, when you reflect back, I think there's always things to learn from it, and there's also a lot of positives to take with you. Obviously when you get to play in the playoffs, it's the best thing in the world, but when you lose out, it's just a tough moment, but every single time you learn new things about yourself. At the same time, if you have success, you have to realize you're just one part of the team and you have to do your job. You can't change the way you are or the way you play the game or the way you react to things off the ice. I think all of those things that happened to me the past few years was a little bit of a humbling moment, especially at the end of the season when we didn't make the playoffs. I think we lost nine out of the last 10 games, so it was a good chance to look in the mirror and get back to working hard. It's just one of those humbling moments."

Goldman: How do you handle the stress knowing that you're considered an elite goaltender asked to play almost all of your team's games?

Rinne: "Well, I mean, I'm absolutely living the dream, so I think I cherish that opportunity and I love that challenge. At the same time, when I go into a season, I obviously look at the schedule, but I try to live it out in short sections throughout the season. I don't really set any goals for myself as far as how many games I want to play. I just focus on short sections, maybe five games at a time, and just focus on building momentum and getting things going for yourself and your team, and then moving along. I think it's a great challenge overall. It's so much fun obviously, especially when things are going well, but even when things aren't going well. Like this year, for myself, it's a big challenge, and at the end of the day, even though it's not so much fun, you still cherish those moments. Hopefully in the future, next season, I'm able to look back and realize that I learned something from it. But I never try to put any extra pressure on myself. I just try to be as good as I can be and try to have a pretty grounded mindset going into the season by taking it in little pieces as we move along."

Goldman: Earlier you talked about still always learning new things. I know you work with Mitch Korn and we talked to him about the mental side of the position. In terms of always being in a state of learning, what has he taught you recently about the mental game?

Rinne: "I think with Mitch, I obviously have worked with him for so long, so I have learned a lot from him and we've had good success and I'm lucky to be working with him. I think with Mitch, the biggest thing is that it's not like a science. It is simple things and you just try to stay in your happy place. Everyone is different, and when I'm at my best, I'm pretty relaxed and still focused. He knows me so well that he can always tell the difference if I'm a little uptight, or if I put too much pressure on my shoulders, he sees it and he can bring me back to being me. He's helped me a lot just to stay even-keeled. You hear that a lot, but I just try to remember how you feel when you're doing well, and what state of mind you're in when you're at your best. You try to learn from that and try to exercise that feeling to be in your natural state of mind when you are in mid-season form or whatever. So you try to stay in your happy place. Sometimes it's hard to put things behind you, but at the same time, the more seasons you play, the more you learn how to do it and how to be ready for another challenge. That's one of the things Mitch is really good at helping me remember."

Goldman: Are there any mental tricks or any insight you can give us in regards to how you manage the highs and lows, or how you approach staying even-keeled?

Rinne: "I kind of have a routine on game days and it starts as soon as I wake up. The whole body is in a game mode, but more than anything it's just a routine and you don't even really have to remind yourself too much. Everything I do, I kind of do it the same way, and after the game I try to give myself that night to think about the game. Sometimes it takes a while to fall asleep, but the next day when I wake up, I try not to think about that game and move on to the next game. Pretty simple things, but I feel like it's still important to go through a game in your head and give yourself some time. If you feel good or angry about the game, it's not wrong to have those feelings. I give myself time to experience those feelings that night, then I move on. I really don't have any tricks or anything like that, just a lot of routines. Usually my routine starts the night before by thinking about the next game and then when I wake up the next morning, it's already game day and everything you do, you don't even have to think about it. You live in your own schedule and it obviously gets easier the more you play. But yeah, I think those are the things I find myself doing often."

Goldman: How important is it to stay disciplined within that routine amidst all of the distractions that come from being an elite NHL goaltender?

Rinne: "I think it's pretty important, but I think more than anything, it's just staying positive. That's when good things happen, and on game days I still talk to media and try not to change anything. I just try to be myself and be laid back. If there's something going wrong or there are delays when traveling, I'm not going to let those things mess up my routine. I try not to take any stress about anything, but at the same time, I try to stay positive and happy. When you're in a good place, good things happen, and you're able to do good things."

Goldman: Was there an experience you had where you weren't happy or positive, and if so, what did you learn from that experience?

Rinne: "I still go through those mixed feelings every single season and there are stretches where things aren't going your way. During those moments, you are tested. It's easy to get angry and easy to feel sorry for yourself, and sure there's a lot of times where you catch yourself being mad and frustrated and sorry for yourself, but at the same time, it's pretty natural. I'm sure everybody goes through these same kind of things. But you try to handle them the right way, and at the end of the day, even though we are individuals in a team sport, you are still on a team, so you try to be a good teammate and do the right things. But it's easier said than done, and it takes work to stay positive and stay happy. You have to face those different feelings almost every day during the season, so it's just how you handle those feelings that matters."

Goldman: How important is it to be honest with yourself and your game?

Rinne: "I think it's really important to realize how you've played, what you're doing in practice, and also off the ice how you handle things. Being honest is really important, because if you realize you're doing something wrong, the sooner the better obviously, because it can hurt you if you start trying to find excuses for why the team isn't playing well. A lot of times, those are the moments when you get yourself in trouble and you start focusing on the wrong things instead of yourself. It's really important to stay honest and reflect on what's happening around you, and also what's happening inside your head."

Goldman: I remember reading about how you did some Yoga training. What did you learn about the mental side of the game from doing Yoga?

Rinne: "My first goal was just to see if it could help my mobility and that kind of physical stuff. But now I've done it for three summers, and while I don't do it every day, it's a part of my off-season training. The more you do it, the more you realize that when you're in the right state of mind, the more your body is willing to do. But when you're stressed out, or mad, or you have a million thoughts in your head, your body doesn't function the way you want it to function. You can learn from those simple things."

Goldman: Everyone knows what it's like to be in the zone. How would you explain it in your own words?

Rinne: "Yeah, it is a hard question, but I think those are the moments when you say after the game you felt you were in it. You notice that feeling after the game, because when you go into the game, you feel good about yourself. Usually it happens during a game when things start going your way and it starts by building up some confidence. You feel big, you feel fast, you feel like the game is slowing down, and you see the puck well. All of those things work together, and so I think it's something that happens naturally. It's a really hard thing to notice in yourself before the game, but in the game you feel it, you feel relaxed, you're in the right frame of mind. You feel like on any given night you're going to win the game, and when things start going your way, your confidence builds up. A lot of times when that happens, it also is kind of contagious and your teammates start feeding off it."

Goldman: How do you personally find ways to dig out from not being confident?

Rinne: "Confidence wise, I had a great learning experience in Milwaukee during my first season in North America. We went all the way to the Calder Cup Finals and it was an unbelievable experience. I had a really good year, and it was my first year playing a lot of games. We went to the finals and played against Hershey and I was playing great. We were up 2-1 and I had a shutout and things were going well, but then all of a sudden I had a bad game and the series was 2-2. I was a young guy and the first time in that situation in North America. So I think they won the series 4-2 and I was never the same after that fourth game. I had a great coach in Claude Noel [Winnipeg], and he was the one who sat me down and saw how I lost my confidence and how I was nervous, and even a bit scared, just to play the next game. He had a great influence on me at the time even though we ended up losing in the finals. Moving forward, he had a big influence on me, just about how to deal with individual games, or how to deal with a bad play, or how to deal with not scaring yourself. I think I learned a lot from that, and obviously there are still moments when I lose my confidence, but I think at this moment I'm better at dealing with those moments. When I remind myself that this is just a hockey game, and we're pretty fortunate just to be playing, it helps. I know it's a cheesy thing to say and it's a cliché, but that's just the way it is. That was a good learning experience for me about confidence. When all of a sudden you have a good season and you're in the finals, you can still totally lose your confidence, and all of a sudden you don't even want to play. I think that was a good experience for me, and I still remember the way I felt, so it's a good reminder."

Goldman: You said you discovered a lot about yourself. So if you were to look back since you started with Nashville, what have you discovered about yourself as an elite athlete that has become an important lesson as a reminder?

Rinne: "A lot of times you have to remind yourself that you have to enjoy the game and have fun. That's when you start having a tough time; when you get too down on yourself or too low. It's so true, you have to enjoy the game. I don't know if I remember any single moment, but I've always learned from the older players just the way they handle themselves at any given moment. As a young player, it's an emotional roller coaster when you let individual games and results kind of define who you are. If you win the game, you're on top of the world, but if you lose, you feel awful. I think in my first few years in Nashville, looking at the older players and how they handled themselves at different times, they were the backbone of the team. I think all of those things help a lot when you're able to spend time with older guys who have been through a lot of the same stuff you have. Just keep your eyes open and always learn from other players. Obviously everyone is different, but I feel like that's what works for me."

Goldman: Besides being pretty laid back and relaxed, you seem to have a simple approach to the mental game. How important is it to keep things simple in a world where more and more goalies are being over-technical?

Rinne: "Yeah, I try to keep things simple, and I've always been so competitive that my only goal is to win games. The technical things never really get into my head. If I'm doing something wrong, I know I can fix it in practice, so I never stress about those things. If I have a sloppy stick or something one night, but we end up winning the game, I don't really worry about it because I know the next day I'll go out with Mitch and work on those things. When you play a lot of games and there's a lot of pressure and stress, you have to be kind to yourself. You have to know the moments when you have to be in a game mode and when you can be relaxed, and I think the sooner you realize that, the easier it gets. It's a long season and a tough grind, so I feel like you can't just live and breathe hockey 24-7. I try to take things pretty simply, but at the same time, there's a lot of processing in my head and in my own thoughts. So I do try to stay relaxed and also have that fire in you, and I think that's my take on keeping things simple."

Goldman: How do you find ways to just play and live in the moment?

Rinne: "I think for myself, it starts when you're passionate about something and you get fired up. But I think it's important to remember that living in the moment is easier said than done. You can't worry about what might happen during the game, or what people might think about you, or anything like that. Everyone is going to go through things like that, and it's just human nature that the more you play and the more you're in different situations like that, the easier it becomes."

Chapter 24
THE PROCESS OF BECOMING

"Flow in the living moment. We are always in a process of becoming and nothing is fixed. Have no rigid system in you, and you'll be flexible to change with the changing." —Bruce Lee

When you consider your skill development as a process rather than a product, you begin to see coaches, teammates, people, game-oriented events and circumstances in a different light. Rather than passing judgment on others, you see their pursuits and actions simply as parts of the journey.

Rather than struggle to make things happen, you begin to step back and watch them unfold, and instead of getting angry when things do not go your way, you look for the lessons that can be learned from every experience you go through.

Similarly, when we consider the art of athletics as a process, we begin to realize that as soon as one goal is achieved another jumps in to take its place. A championship team enjoys their success but knows that the stakes have been raised and even greater things will be expected of them in the future.

It is this ever-expanding process of goal-setting that propels committed athletes to the next level. However, it is a process that cannot be rushed. If we try to meet our goals without doing the necessary legwork, we will only struggle with too much too soon.

Although "any team can beat any team on any given night," ultimately it is the team that plays intelligently and deliberately that will come out on top. The team that focuses on each step and covers each aspect of the game in its entirety will be more successful than one that steps on the ice expecting to win out of sheer determination.

Furthermore, the individual athlete that gives equal attention to all aspects of his position will advance his game quicker and more deliberately than one who only works on a single area. The will to win is only part of the equation – focusing on the actual process of winning is the other part.

The Tao Te Ching says, "All of life is a movement toward perfection" but it does not say a meeting of perfection. This is because our earthly journey does not include the meeting of perfection. As long as we are alive, we will continue to pursue that which we desire. But when one desire has been met, another will take its place. It is this phenomenon that keeps the life force pumping through us.

Even those goalies at the top of their game, the best of the best, continue to strive and wish for even more. Whether it be in their professional lives or personal lives, they have the desire and motivation to keep moving forward. They do not stagnate.

Therefore, the lesson about the process of becoming is simple. Each day, take one small step toward perfection, but realize that you will never get there. Take care of the small things and focus on the details and the big things will take care of themselves.

Master each step along the way with care and intent. For as we all know, life is a journey, not a destination.

-Valley

Chapter 25

TALKING WITH MITCH KORN

Author's Note: You've heard his name mentioned a few times before in this book. You've also likely heard about his success as an NHL goalie coach for more than 20 years. But now you have a chance to hear some of the most exclusive and rare insights from the wizard, Mitch Korn. He has coached Dominik Hasek, Tomas Vokoun, Pekka Rinne, Chris Mason, and so many more to the level of being elite, making him the ultimate interview for The Mental Warrior. This is more than a treat, it is pure gold. Enjoy the wisdom that comes from this amazing interview with two current NHL goalie coaches!

Valley: In your experience, what makes an elite goalie better than the average NHL goalie?

Korn: "Right now, and even a few years ago, the skill between NHL goalie number-one and number-60 isn't that dramatic. Think about it. Maybe the top guy is a little bigger, a little faster or a little stronger. But it's not that. What separates guy number-one from number-60 is largely mental. And it's not only the capacity to handle the mental pressures or anxiety and key moments in games, but it's also the mental capability of recognizing patterns, reading and reacting, and the senses that they have to have to be successful. There's so much that occurs between the ears that really end up separating number-one from number-60, way more than the physical body."

Valley: What are the mental traits that you see in all the top goalies that make them elite? What does the process look like for them?

Korn: "That's hard because a number of guys have been very successful for different reasons. Sometimes it's skating ability, sometimes it's their size. But in general, first and foremost, all of these guys absolutely love to play. You have to throw them off the ice some days in order to manage their ice time. In a long season of 82 games, with as much as our top guys play, we need to manage their ice time. They'd stay out there all day if we let them. I've coached some guys that were more talented than some of the top guys, but they didn't love to play. They didn't love to compete. They didn't love or embrace the challenge, but the elite guys love it. Secondly, they put in the work. When you get paid for something, it's considered work. But when you go out on the ice, that's not work. You love to play and it's no longer work. It requires effort that is beyond the average person's imagination, but the effort isn't work. And when the effort isn't work, it is embraced way more because it is so gratifying. I think the names in your book – Vokoun is one of them and Mason is one of them and certainly Pekka is one of them – they all absolutely love to play and they love everything involved with the game. They love their equipment, they're educated, they know what other guys in the league are doing, and they're goalie geeks."

Valley: So we look at these successful guys, and I wonder what obstacles have you had to see them overcome? Have any of these successful guys seen nerves get in the way? Is there any other mental or emotional attribute that the successful guys have?

Korn: "I look at a guy like Vokoun, who has OCD. At one time it was becoming debilitating for him because he was paralyzed by it. We actually diagnosed him and got him on meds and while it reared its ugly head, it gave him a chance to succeed. I remember hearing stories about Dominik Hasek being with Chicago where he almost headed back to the Czech Republic. I never asked him about that, but he had a really good career in Buffalo. There was a time where the Sabres traded for Grant Fuhr and Hasek was left exposed in the expansion draft that year, and I think it was Ottawa and Tampa Bay that came in and they both had a chance to pick him up, but they didn't. It was the next year that Fuhr hurt his knee and Hasek went on to win his first Vezina Trophy. I remember when Vokoun was traded and Mason was the anointed starting goalie, but he didn't handle that very well. He cared so much that he put enormous pressure on himself and no longer enjoyed playing. It changed his outlook. He was no longer the underdog; the guy battling to play. He was 'the guy' and he couldn't handle it at that point. It wasn't until he got to St. Louis and had another crack at it that he learned to manage those feelings, those expectations. It's not easy."

Valley: So let's talk about a guy like Hasek. What made him so special? Obviously he had a ton of skill on the ice. But what made him so elite?

Korn: "He was extremely competitive. From the physical skill standpoint, he was extremely quick. He had lightning legs, he was contortable and he was able to seal the ice very well. But we had a goalie who was his backup that was actually a better athlete than Dom. His name was Andrei Trefilov. He could jump higher, run faster, and was actually even more flexible in some ways. But we never heard of Trefilov, did we? We heard of Hasek. And why? Because Hasek had a very short memory. He'd give up a goal and it was gone. He never fretted about it – he didn't worry about those things. They did a story on him at one time and they found out he was a genius. He tested extremely high for IQ and would have been in the Mensa Club if he tried to join. And I think that genius translated to things like his ability to read and react to the game, and knowing what would happen next. His composure is what allowed him to use that information in a positive way and not panic. When Dom first got to Buffalo, I can still remember him playing an electronic chess game, and that translated on the ice because he was always one or two steps ahead of other players. Not that he showed his hand, but he understood – like maybe Gretzky did in his position – what was more than likely going to happen next, and it gave him a leg up on everyone else. As far as mental toughness, he never really fretted about much. If he was North American, we would have called him eccentric because he really had no real sense of time. He was late all the time and was always disheveled, and as coaches we know those kinds of guys, they really don't fret or worry. He was just alive, so nothing really got in his way. Fuhr was similar to that, and I used to say that Grant was a 14-year-old adult. Not in his maturity, but how many 14-year-olds get nervous? Kids don't get nervous. They play and have fun. The pressure from the crowds or their parents or contracts or drafts and scholarships aren't there. That's how Grant played, which is probably why he would make more 'big saves' late in a game than almost anybody in his career. Not that he had a great save percentage or goals against in today's era, but it always seemed like when the game was on the line, he knew how to make the big saves because the pressure never paralyzed him in any way shape or form."

Valley: Obviously those guys had their fair share of bad games. How would Hasek react after giving up four or five?

Korn: "No different than Brodeur or Roy or the other greats. I always say that true starting goalies never have two bad games in a row. The reason for that is simple: those guys that I mentioned never competed with their backup, they competed with themselves. They always challenged themselves and they embraced the opportunity to be the guy, the man, the difference-maker. They loved it and enjoyed it and that's what they thrived on. Some people get paralyzed by the pressure, but elite goalies get motivated by it."

Valley: Everyone knows that you couldn't score on Hasek in practice. Was he always that competitive?

Korn: "From the minute I met him, he was always extremely competitive on the ice. Off the ice, he was a bit more laid back. I guess he got real competitive in cards when they played, and he was also very competitive against the chess game he played. But he really got to show his real competitive nature in front of the crowds. My favorite Hasek story came during his first year with the team, and this is when I knew he was special. I was standing in the corner to Dom's left on his glove side. He was in the net and we were on a smaller ice surface. He had begun a little competitive battle with a guy named Donald Audette. Dom hated when pucks were in the net, and Donald liked to push his buttons, so they had this little war that began. I can still remember the play clearly. I'm standing to his left, Donald is to Dom's right and in line to roll through a drill. A line is coming down on Dom 3-on-2, he's at the top of the crease, and from the right corner, Donald snapped one at the empty net behind Dom. I'm watching this, and I actually got nervous because I saw the puck coming towards the crease and was afraid it would come behind him, right by the post, and maybe hit me. I'm watching this, and then suddenly I see Dom turn to his right, and in one motion, knock the puck right out of the air with the paddle of his stick, then quickly turn back and stop the 3-on-2 after that. I knew immediately at that moment that this guy was special. First of all, he was aware of what Donald was doing out of the corner of his right eye. Secondly, he had the eye-hand coordination required to knock that thing out of the air, which was pretty special. Thirdly, obviously he played the 3-on-2 right away and made the transition and stopped it."

Valley: So is Hasek a guy that was born and raised that way, or was it something he learned? Did you experience a maturity change in his time in Buffalo?

Korn: "I think it's a little of everything. We all talk about nature versus nurture, and I think there are certainly components that are learned, and certainly components that they learn themselves through the School of Hard Knocks, or they learned because they played with a goalie partner. Even though he was very competitive, Eddy Belfour took it to the next level, and he played with Belfour in Chicago, so that had to have a positive impact on Dom. And yet there are things Belfour did that Dom told me he didn't want to be like. Between periods, you couldn't talk to Eddy. But with Dom, you could talk to him like it was the middle of the afternoon, because he was able to turn it off and turn it back on. That would be nurture; the experiences and guys you play with. But there's also nature, which is inherent in you. I don't think in all our coaching, you can ever make a non-competitive guy competitive. You'll never make a non-killer a killer. And so there needs to be some of that coming from inside a person. Once in a while we can light the fuse, but it only stays lit for a little while. The elite goalies can keep the fuse lit all by themselves."

Valley: Does Pekka have the same qualities as Hasek? The competitiveness? What makes Rinne so good?

Korn: "I would say the competitiveness is definitely there. Somebody once said to me about Rinne, that he would rather get hit in the head with a chair than give up a goal in practice. They never take a minute off, they never give up on a puck, they battle until the battle is over. When pucks are in the net, they dislike it. Peks is very competitive. He battles on every puck and that's the internal, or I refer to it as the emotional part of the game. I think that competitive nature is more emotional because it's less controllable. They're more inherent. But when you talk about Dom and Pekka, they both have the uncanny ability to know what's happening next, they both have phenomenal hand-eye coordination, and they read patterns. Hockey is a game of patterns, and the faster you recognize a pattern, the easier it is to stop the puck. Both of those guys had an unbelievable ability to know what's happening next. They know where people are. There's 10 people on the ice in their zone at any given moment, and they know where they all are. Those two guys probably track the puck better than anyone I've seen. And their ability to read pucks off the stick, which is a pattern as well, one that over time you recognize, and well, they know where pucks are going. They track pucks to their body and find pucks in traffic, they connect the dots because they understand the game with the parts that are missing when they can't see the puck. They were so special that way, and that's one of the key reasons why they are so special."

Valley: That's so true because you don't find it in a ton of goalies, but I look at Kari and his hockey IQ is so high. He'll come in before a game and talk about setups on the power play and when to expect one-timers and he's calculating these things with all of this information.

Korn: "Remember earlier in this conversation we talked about guys that are goalie geeks? They're educated and knowledgeable and recognize the patterns and know who they're playing against. If you were a stock broker and were going to invest in a company, you were going to know everything about that company. You'd know the CEO and the CFO and the balance sheets and the debt and the new products before you invest in them. Goalies need to know that stuff too in order to be effective. Now I've coached guys that don't want to know, and so do you. Even when we do the shootout and we teach our shooters how to score, they're overwhelmed and they get friggin' paralyzed. They don't want to know, they just want to react. One guy says, 'I just want to use my instincts.' I said, where do you think those instincts come from? They're developed inside you from your experiences. You didn't just wake up as a two-year-old being able to play the piano. You have to learn how to play! Same with hockey, you develop those instincts. I give goalies knowledge to update their instincts, but they have to be able to use it, and some goalies don't want that. I believe knowledge is power, and the more knowledge you have, when used properly, in theory, the more power you have over your opponent."

Valley: One of the things that we see with younger goalies is that they over-prepare. If we look at morning skates, yes Pekka is focused and Kari is laser-focused for the game, but it revs up during the day, but they're very careful that it's not revved up too high too early. What are some of the things that you see with that, with young guys over-preparing and being mentally exhausted by the time the game begins?

Korn: "My saying is, 'Don't play the game before we play the game.' And as players age, they start to figure out what works for them. For you it might be music, for this guy it might be a racquetball, for this guy it might be a jog, everyone is a little different in preparation. But I have tried very hard in every goalie I've gotten, to not let them get introverted in the morning of a game, or even at times leading up to a game. I think when you do, and you play a long season, even in a 32-game college season, and you're a #1 goalie, at some point you will explode. So I don't want them, for no better term, burying their head, shaking their head, trying to get ready to play by psyching up. I think that's all a giant façade. You are successful at every level when you play on skill. You elevate that skill with emotion. The mental aspects we talk about is a skill - being able to control what you think and how you control what's going on in your head during the game is a skill. And then there's the emotion; the adrenaline that takes it to the next level is like a turbo boost for your skill. That's why you see great performances at big moments. Great goalies turn in great performances because they're on turbo boosts."

Valley: If I look at one of the best pieces of advice I ever got, it came from Curtis Joseph. He said you can prepare all day for a game. And you can go out in warm-ups and feel fantastic and the first shot goes off a player's butt or skate and goes in. Now what do you do? Or, you could have had a pre-game skate where things weren't going well, you go out to warm-up, you don't feel right, but all of a sudden you pitch a shutout. So his bottom line was, just relax, play the game when the game is played, and control what you can control. For me, I didn't get that advice until later in my career from him, and it was really helpful because I tried too hard. I tried to prepare too much, when all I needed to do was relax and play the game, let it unfold, and let it happen like it's going to happen. You're going to have great nights, and you're going to have nights that aren't great.

Korn: "And there's no correlation between morning skates, or no correlation from how you felt today in school. I have been watching morning skates and games for 22 years. I've stood at center ice and the head coach goes, 'Wow is he sharp. He's going to be awesome tonight,' and he totally stinks. Or a coach will go, 'Oh my god, are you sure you want to play this guy tonight?!' and he plays great. There is zero correlation. The game is its own entity."

Valley: The other thing we should talk about is building upon that. When you have a rookie goalie that's coming into play, whether the NHL or AHL or even at a younger level, what are the pieces of advice that you give to that goalie? We don't want to get them over-thinking, so what do you tell them when they're getting that big chance?

Korn: "You have to love to play and you have to enjoy the moment. I think by enjoying it, you lessen the pressure just a little bit and you relax just enough to not be tense and paralyzed. The best goalies are agile, quick and fluid like Jell-O. But when you have too much induced pressure, you're like cement and you can't play like that. So that's my first piece of advice for goalies; enjoy this. There are a million goalies that wish they were where you are today. Second, worry about what you can control. There are so many things that happen that you can't control. I often say that every goalie is playing the game, and your brain is your computer. We use practices to program your computer. We don't do it in games. Our job as goalie coaches is to help you program the computer in practice. For every action, we have an equal and opposite reaction. That's what we do as goalies, we react. In a game, we just have to recognize what's going on, and then pull the right program. In games, it's purely reaction. It's having been trained, and then you react. You recognize the pattern and pull the correct program so there's no delay or over-thinking, just reacting. And so if you're relaxed, you react way better than if you're tense. There are delays when you're tense."

Valley: If you're tense, you just can't do it. Everything is slowed down.

Korn: "We talk about being in turbo mode, and we take those skills, and the adrenaline allows you to be faster, not slower. Your adrenaline needs to be an asset, not your kryptonite. That's why you see great guys have great games at great moments. They embrace the moment and love being on stage. Maybe it's a degree of ego. I said before that Dom loved being on stage, and we've all heard the stories of different goalies' egos. They love being the center of attention and the focal point. As long as it's managed well, if that's what drives their engine, go for it. It makes them better and the team better. As long as they don't stand up when it's over and say, "me, me, it's me, I'm awesome!" But if they can use it internally to help them be better, so be it.

We all have a little ego in there. Great goalies want to make a significant and positive difference every time they play. We're both goalie coaches. What do we want to do? We want to make a significant difference every time we coach. That's why we've done it for a long time. That's what great goalies do, they can sustain it, and they make a significant difference every time they play."

Valley: I look at Richard Bachman. He is probably one of the most mentally tough goalies I've ever met in my life and ever seen. You look at the things he's had to overcome; he's a smaller goalie, and there are so many things he's had to overcome in his life to get to where he is now.

Korn: "He found mechanisms to overcome the weaknesses. If you were blind, what improves? Your hearing and your other senses. There are compensations being made. So in his case, he reads the play unbelievably well. He's quick as a cat, he's tough as nails and he has become tough because he was probably told a thousand times while growing up that he's not going to make it."

Valley: One of the ways he approaches each NHL game, he never has any fear or anxiety. He's relaxed, composed, and he looks at every day as a great opportunity. We're playing a meaningless game against the Blues last season and they're trying to capture the President's Trophy so they have a good lineup. We played a bunch of our younger guys, but he looked at the rosters and said, "Gosh this is a great opportunity." Or the very first time he got called up, he was called into Chicago and although he wasn't playing, I went up to him and said, "Hey, you ready to go tonight?" and he said, "Absolutely. I'm always ready, I'm excited." So he never has that fear or that pit in his stomach that he might get embarrassed. He embraces each opportunity as if it's a chance to grow or show that he can play in the NHL. Fear just doesn't enter the equation.

Korn: "Attitude determines altitude. He doesn't get paralyzed and that's his mechanism. There are guys that are bigger or more skilled that might possess some of the negatives, but they can survive on their skills and size. But they'll never be great until they get the mental part in order."

Valley: He never lets a tough practice or a bad goal affect him. It goes back to what we said earlier, he's just in the moment and he plays and doesn't let his anxiousness or fear or lack of controlling his emotions drown him.

Korn: "Our coach in Nashville has a great saying. He says, "There are a lot of players who get in their own way because they talk themselves out of stuff, or because they are angry at something, and they let it get in their way. If they have issues outside of the rink, that gets in their way. The best guys are able to turn everything and all the anxiety and distractions off, and just play the game when it's time to play the game."

Valley: How do you prevent anxiety when you see a young guy getting anxious or over-trying?

Korn: "When you over-try, the game goes too fast, and you're unable to keep up. That's the beauty of sports psychologists and that's why we're lucky for the business we're in that we have access to those kinds of people. They have a variety of strategies, from breathing to imagery, to try and help give these guys strategies. Even in-game ones like water on your face, rebooting the computer, and finding what works for you. I know a goalie that would actually put his girlfriend's perfume on the cuff of his wristband, and he would take the catching glove off and smell it to help him re-focus in games because it was a calming effect for him. It sounds bizarre, but that was a recommendation of a high-level sports psych guy. That was one of the strategies this guy used to help the goalie calm down in the game. The disadvantage was that you needed a whistle to do it, because you couldn't do it while things were going on. I think by the time a guy gets to you or me, they've weeded themselves out, and they haven't gotten that far. Even at the minor hockey level, they get weeded out, or they quit playing because it's not fun or comfortable or enjoyable. So we're lucky, we get the cream of the crop, and some of the issues that might occur are issues goalies may grow into them, not grow out of them, as the stakes increase."

Valley: Why do goaltenders get better with age?

Korn: "Patterns. It's a game of experience. But if you break down the save process, what matters is how quickly you make the decisions, and how right you are in making those decisions by recognizing the situation and the patterns. As we age, we all mellow, and that little bit of mellowing out is a good thing in goal. Don't get me wrong, we need adrenaline. But we also need to be able to slow things down. We talk about patterns, we talk about patience, and as we get more experience we recognize them faster and gain more composure. We know what's coming and we see it over and over again."

Valley: Why do some guys play their best when they are sick?

Korn: "Because they're far more focused and they bear down. You subconsciously say that you're not healthy, you don't want to get embarrassed, so I better crank it up. I never played pro hockey, but I can tell you as a youngster, I too played my best games sick. It just seems that you conserve energy, and that's probably more important than anything. You're not wasting energy on things you can't control, and you're ultra-focused because you know you have to be, because things aren't feeling perfect."

Valley: Last question. You get to say one thing to a goalie before he goes out on the ice for a big game. What do you say?

Korn: "Oh wow. You know what? I think it depends on the goalie. If we're good goalie coaches, we know what buttons to push. I've coached guys where it would probably make sense to say, "If you win tonight, your next contract will be worth at least \$2 million more." And to him, that would be the most ultimate motivating factor. But I would never say that to a different guy that isn't motivated by money. So I think it's based on the guy, but in general, if I had to come up with a closing statement for the readers, I would say: enjoy it, embrace it. This will be a blast!"

Chapter 26
THE END OF THE BEGINNING

"Ever since I was a child, I have had this instinctive urge for expansion and growth. To me, the function and duty of a quality human being is the sincere and honest development of one's potential." —Bruce Lee

Now that you've come to the conclusion of this book, we hope you're ready to begin a new chapter in your own life as a goaltender. Filled with many morsels of wisdom regarding the position, you should have plenty of new information to ponder and digest as you continue to reflect upon your current state of development.

This should be an exciting time.

It's the chance for a rebirth, a revolution of your own evolution. It's a chance to grow stronger, gain more experience, and perform at a higher level.

But just like we stressed in the introduction, remember that the art of becoming an elite goaltender is a time-consuming process of maturing and molding into a higher state of consciousness. It does not happen overnight.

Just like the iron sword is forged in fire and pounded into perfect form by the blacksmith, so too is your psyche and mental approach forged in the heat of many goaltending battles. Take each game as an opportunity to express yourself in a balanced and relaxed manner. Continue to embrace the fact that failures are necessary to achieving that flow; they allow you to learn more about the same type of "patterns" that Mitch Korn mentioned at the end of his interview.

So as you move forward with the arrow of time, never be afraid to fail and never be afraid to try something new, because it is through change that we truly learn. At the same time, always strive to analyze your game and your mental approach with honesty. If you can't be honest with yourself, you will never be able to determine which areas need work and which areas are already solid. You will stagnate and you will fall behind.

"Everything you do, if not in a relaxed state will be done at a lesser level than you are proficient. Thus the tensed expert marksman will aim at a level less than his student."—Bruce Lee

As you learned throughout this book, when it comes to achieving the flow that goalies so desperately seek, one of the keys is learning how to play with a relaxed state of mind.

When relaxed, we are worry-free, clear-headed and focused on the puck. And when we achieve those things, we play in the moment and we don't hinder our own proficiencies. With so many things causing stress and anxiety in today's society, the only way to truly escape those obstacles is to think less.

One of the ways a goaltender learns how to think less is by establishing and perfecting their own unique routine. Regardless of what is going on in your personal life, your ability to get into the rhythm of that routine fully prepares you for the task at hand without having to worry about all of those external pressures.

Routine is the essence of preparation – it allows you to find a comfortable space in your mind and stay occupied and focused on the different tasks needed to help you enter a state of true clarity and readiness.

But beyond all of these tools, tricks, interviews, teaching points and words of advice, we'd like to impart one final and far-reaching piece of wisdom that encompasses all others.

The answers you seek to any question regarding the position is already deep inside of you. Find those answers by first discovering more about who you are. Discover more about who you are by gaining more experience whenever you can. Gain more experience whenever you can by working hard, living in the moment, embracing the opportunity to play the greatest position in sports, and most importantly, by *having fun*.

For as Valley says, "You play some of the best hockey in your life when you're happy."

47789458R00108

Made in the USA
Middletown, DE
02 September 2017